Self-Defense – Feel Secure at All Times

Dedication

I dedicate this book to my former trainers Jeff Espinous and Paul Vunak. From Paul, I have learned most of my knowledge from his videos, but had the honor to see him live in Munich and learn from his students Tom Cruse, Roy Harris and Michael Grüner. I was with Jeff as a member of the EKAEF/IKAEF for several years. Both are excellent trainers in the art of effective self-defense and I can heartily recommend taking part in both of their seminars. Without the knowledge I have gained from them, this book would not have been possible.

Many thanks to both of them for everything that I have been able to learn from them.

Warning

This book contains some techniques that can be very dangerous and must only be practiced under the supervision of a qualified trainer or instructor. The author and the publishers cannot be held responsible for any injuries that might ensue. All the exercises should be carried out using a blunt exercise knife (made of aluminum or wood) or by using a padded stick. Both participants in the exercises should wear protective glasses for their own safety. In order to avoid injuries, attacks to the face using a knife or a stick should not be carried out.

Note:

This book has been written using exclusively the male form of the personal pronoun. Of course, for reasons of simplicity this should be understood to include the female form as well.

Christian Braun

Self-Defense

Feel Secure at All Times

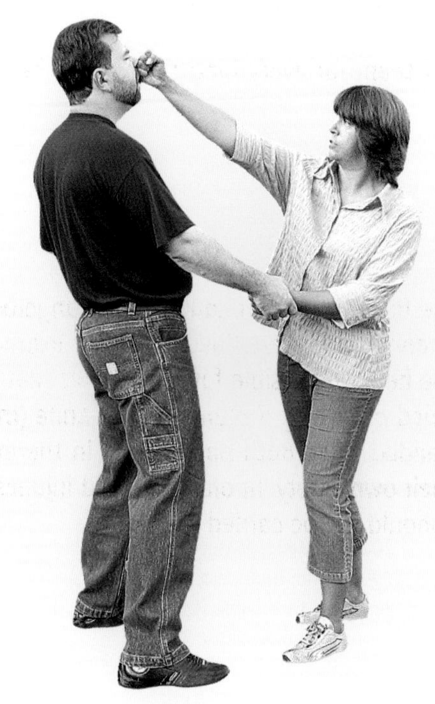

Meyer & Meyer Sport

Original title: Selbstverteidigung – Techniken, die wirklich helfen

British Library Cataloguing in Publication Data
A catalogue record for this book is available from the British Library

Christian Braun: Self-Defense – Feel Secure at All Times
Maidenhead: Meyer & Meyer Sport (UK) Ltd., 2009
ISBN: 978-1-84126-246-8

Aachen, Adelaide, Auckland, Budapest, Cape Town, Graz, Indianapolis, Maidenhead, New York, Olten (CH), Singapore, Toronto
Member of the World
Sports Publishers' Association (WSPA)
www.w-s-p-a.org
Printed and bound by: B.O.S.S Druck und Medien GmbH, Germany
ISBN: 978-1-84126-246-8
E-Mail: verlag@m-m-sports.com
www.m-m-sports.com

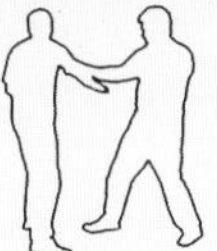

Contents

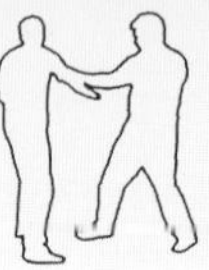

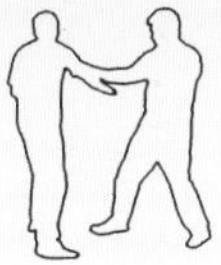

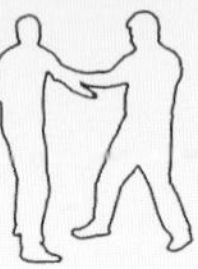

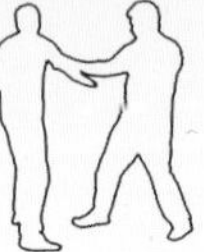

Foreword

You have bought this book in order to learn about the theme of self-defense. Perhaps you are a martial arts sportsman looking for concepts and techniques for your training. Perhaps you are simply an ordinary person who would like to learn a bit more about the subject and to learn a few effective defense techniques and ways of dealing with such problems so that you can survive an attack or even avoid one. Maybe you are a man, who, for example, fears being attacked in a bar by another man. And then again you may be a woman looking for tips to counter sexual harassment by men.

This book can offer the martial arts follower concepts, training methods, techniques and combinations for self-defense. It also offers the man in the street techniques and ways of reacting against attacks. For the women there are lots of tips regarding ways to react and techniques aimed at avoiding sexual harassment.

In the first part of the book, the various dangerous situations are described together with ways of reacting in these situations. In the 'Practical Section' you will find combinations of actions against fistfights in the street. In this section I have also taken the trouble to go through how you can hold an attacker down and bite him before he gets to his feet and, in panic and screaming with pain, makes his getaway. There are descriptions of scenes in a bar including concepts and techniques to play down the seriousness of the situation. Defense against armed attackers with a stick (but also a baseball bat, knife and pistol) and defense on the ground are also covered. A further section deals with the use of everyday objects (for example, newspapers, books, ballpoint pens and keys) as aids for self-defense.

I have been dealing with this subject intensively for more than 20 years and this has taken up a large part of my life. Now I want to pass the knowledge I have gained on to you via this book.

For several years now, I have been offering seminars in self-defense, especially for women. Besides other things, I have repeated the content of these seminars here in this book. In 1996, I got to be in contact with Thomas (Tom) Cruze, the former Vice-President of Progressive Fighting Systems. Tom totally changed my way of thinking about self-defense. For starters, there were no individual techniques in the foreground, rather only the concept of self-defense.

At that time, I also learned PFS (a mixture of the concept of Jeet Kune Do and Filipino Martial Arts) and I am now an instructor under Paul Vunak. Amongst other things, Paul had been an instructor for the Navy Seals (US Special Forces unit). I was able to adopt some good ideas from him for the theme of self-defense.

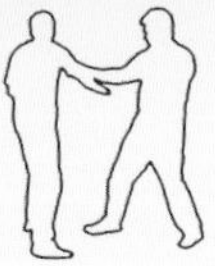

Furthermore, I was taught over several years by Jeff Espinous, the founder of the Kali-Sikaran. I am also an instructor (Guro) in his organization. Jeff is one of the best self-defense instructors that I know. There is then, of course, on top of all this the influence of my Luta-Livre teacher – Andreas Schmidt.

Having practiced Jiu-Jitsu now for 25 years or more, I was able to be trained by many excellent instructors. It is not possible to name them all here. However, I would just like to mention representatively for this discipline Bernd Hillebrand, Joe Thumfart, Ralf Pfeiffer and Herbert Frese.

May I wish you lots of fun going through the lessons and I hope that you never have to put what you have learned into practice.

Bruce Lee, one of the greatest Martial Arts fighter of all time once said, "Absorb what is useful." I commend this saying to the reader as he goes on his way.

Frankenthal, April 2008
Christian Braun

Acknowledgements

At this juncture, above all, I would like to thank all the trainers I have trained with in the last few years and who have allowed me to improve my knowledge in weaponry. These are Jeff Espinous, Johann Skalberg and Timm Blashke. All three are excellent fighters and instructors and have my full recommendation.

Furthermore I would like to thank the following Masters, who I was either able to work with personally or learn from their videos and books: These include Mike Inay, Bob Breen, Dan Inosanto, Joachim Almeria, Paul Vunak, Simone Schloetels, Bernd Hillebrand, Joe (Joachim) Thumfart, Andreas Schmidt, Tom Cruze and Hock Hochheim.

For their support in helping me to write this book, I would like to thank my students Robert Zawis, Gunther Hatzenbühler, my friend and student Gabi Rogall-Zelt, Jessica Rogall (photo work) and my friend and training partner, Waldemar Wodarz.

My friend, Gabi Rogall-Zelt has spent many years as a dog-handler and has provided me with a number of valuable tips regarding defense against dogs attacks as well as helping put this book together (photo work and editing).

I am grateful to Mr. K. Tsavelis of the Hellas restaurant in Mutterstadt (Germany) in allowing us to use the bar scene photos in the section entitled 'Self-Defense – Special Situations.'

A EVERYDAY TIPS AND TRICKS FOR EVERYONE

Let me emphasize that I'm not an attorney or a policeman and that my judicial knowledge is pretty basic. If you need to have more information about the rules in this book, then please read a law book or ask an attorney. Similarly, my medical knowledge is also a little thin and for deeper questions about this, may I refer you to a doctor.

1 Fighting Back Begins in the Head

You can take part in the very best course on self-defense, learn to do a martial art or own the most effective weapon, but that won't help you at all in a self-defense situation, as long as you are not prepared to use the weapon or techniques you've learned. If you are not prepared to use an aid such as, for example, an irritant, then you don't need to carry this around with you, because the attacker might simply use it against you himself.

1.1 The best three techniques for defense

Run away

Run away

Run away

If you can run away, this is not cowardice, rather it's clever. If it is only you that is involved and you don't have to help anyone then, when you have a chance, run away as fast as you can.

Even when perhaps you could have won the fight, it could have negative results:

- The attacker breaks your nose, gives you a black eye or knocks one of your teeth out. To get the nose back in order means a very unpleasant operation that I myself have already experienced. Losing a tooth is also quite bad and amongst other things, it is costly. If the attacker has no means of support then you have to bear the costs yourself.
- The attacker wounds you and you have to get stitches.
- In the attack your clothing has been dirtied and perhaps even ripped.
- People who were present and act as witnesses later in court could have seen the situation differently than you, and they blame you, thus making trouble for you later on.

My former instructor Jeff Espinous once said to me, "If you run, you will win, otherwise you will be the asshole of the day and for what? For nothing!" Need I say more?

2 Should You Defend Yourself?

In a court it would be expected that someone who practices a martial art has to demonstrate that he does not seek a conflicting situation. Because he has many years of experience in the martial arts, he should advise the attacker what he can do because of his special ability.

I personally think this advice is inadvisable, because the attacker has sought you out with intent. Me, I don't look for a fight; where possible I try to defuse the conflict verbally and if this is not successful, I certainly look to employ the best chances for my defense.

Someone who practices martial arts and trains in 'only' self-defense techniques, never taking part in a competition fight, is to my mind far inferior to a street hooligan. The martial arts athlete has probably never been hit in the face by a person. It can be expected that the athlete will use only a few of the defense possibilities out of all the techniques he has learned. The fact that the athlete, himself, could be in a fearful state of panic is seemingly overlooked. I have been practicing various kinds of martial arts for well over 25 years now, and I have successfully taken part in competitions throughout this time. Despite this, I reckon that I would also be very afraid when suddenly several dangerous looking men started to attack me.

Someone who doesn't know anything about self-defense will be even more afraid. He has to know that the fierceness of the defense techniques must not be greater than the techniques used in the attack, that is, use 'no excess of force' or 'the minimum of force'. Attack and defense should be relative to one another. As soon as the attacker stops or is rendered incapable, then the defensive actions should also end. Any further defensive action could be construed as use of excessive force and could bring a charge of guilty in a court.

The defense technique chosen is also dependent on the defender's constitution and also that of the attacker. If a man weighing 100 kg attacks a woman weighing 60 kg then the woman has to use relatively more forceful techniques than when a 100 kg man attacks another weighing the same.

If, in a court, the more forceful technique can be justified then there is a chance that you won't be punished for the action.

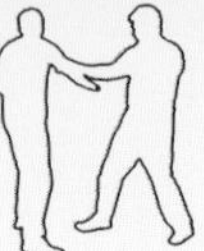

Example:

A policeman gives a person who is resisting arrest a black eye. That person then brings a charge against the policeman. The officer justifies the black eye, saying that the roadway was slippery and a lever throw could have eventually broken the person's arm as he slipped down. The person needs to use a vehicle regularly. A black eye is healed within a week while a broken arm would take much longer and with other implications. The policeman would thus not be punished.

The combinations described in this book show a split second picture of an attack. It is also assumed that one has been attacked by a person who meant it. The suggested defensive combinations are very effective, but as a result this means the attacker will almost always be injured by them (sometimes even seriously).

Therefore, here again is the tip:

As a general rule, avoid a confrontation. If this is not possible, try to resolve the issue verbally. Forceful defense techniques should always be the last resort.

2.1 Attack and defense should be relative to one another

Different countries have different laws. For example, in Germany, the defense against an attack must be relative to that attack. If someone clouts your ear, you cannot kick him back in the genitals. There are also differences in your reaction regarding when and where you are attacked. There is a difference if you have been grabbed by the arm in a shopping mall during the day or if you have been attacked at 2 in the morning by a burglar in your apartment. During the daytime in the shopping mall there are lots of people around who could help you – at night there is nobody to help and therefore it is safer to use a more forceful technique to defend yourself.

2.2 The attack must be directly imminent

If someone is standing in front of you and, for example, yells, "I'm going to stab you!" and reaches inside his jacket, then there is a good chance he will pull out a knife. Thus an attack is imminent. In German law, it states that an attack has to be *"at that moment in time"* or *"be prevailing,"* that is, it must coincide with the threat. You don't have to wait now until he has actually pulled the knife out of his jacket, and you can react by, for example, carrying out a poke with the fingers into his eyes. The same applies if, for example, a man says to a woman "It's your turn now!" She then doesn't have to wait until he has dropped his pants and can go ahead by carrying out a technique such as a jab at the eyes, the creation of pressure in the ears by slapping them with the hands or a similar technique.

Example:

If your bike has been stolen and you meet up with the culprit 10 minutes later, you may not start to attack him because no attack is actually happening at that moment. You have to notify the law, who will take the matter in hand.

2.3 The attack must be unlawful

In order to make a charge of guilty stick, then the attack must be against the law, that is, if you provoke the 'attacker' and insult him and he, in turn, reacts by striking you, then defense from your point of view is no longer counted as 'self-defense'. In such an event you will most certainly have problems in a court case.

2.4 Always watch out

If you are continually watching out then, in many cases, you can avoid the worst. In places where you are not comfortable, I compare my personal behavior to that of a dog. A dog is forever twitching its ears listening to every sound, especially if it is not feeling secure. You should react like this when you are, for example, in an indoor parking lot. If you are unsuspecting and have been subject to a surprise attack, then the shock of being placed in such a situation lasts much longer than when you have been on the watch.

When in buildings like this, make sure you know where the exits are, so that you know which way to run to get away.

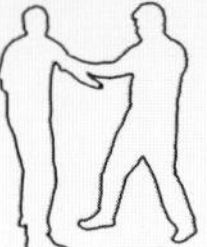

3 Don't Attack the Following Persons

- Children
- Disabled persons
- Drunks

With all of the three groups mentioned, it is assumed that an adult defender is more than a match against these persons so that in such cases he should not undertake any form of defense. If a drunken attacker weighing 120 kg assaults you, the judge in Germany would expect you to get out of the way. Forceful defense in such an event could have the consequence of leading to a criminal prosecution.

Even a teacher is not allowed to employ any defense techniques when attacked by youths. This could also lead to a criminal prosecution.

4 What to Do After the Assault

It is obvious that you would rather go home after such an attack, but you shouldn't do this, because important evidence could be lost that could help you later in a court case. Particularly in the case of a rape, it is important that the female victim doesn't take a shower in order to wash the 'dirt' away. Far better to place a complaint against the perpetrator and secure the evidence of sperm, hair as well as traces of skin under the fingernails, so that a genetic 'fingerprint' can be established.

After making the complaint, you should have a doctor establish the extent of your injuries. At a later date it will be very difficult to obtain ample proof of the facts regarding the injuries.

As a woman, if you have been harassed at work, then you should inform the female work representative or supervisor. These people are there to help you.

5 What Should You Consider Saying When Making a Complaint?

You should consider what information you use to notify those needing to know, that is, consider whether you mention that you practice a martial art or attend regular self-defense courses. At the very least do not resort to technical terms.

Example:

"I carried out a Zuki (punch with the fist) to the opponent's stomach and turned around and threw the attacker to the ground with a Seoi-nage (shoulder throw)."

The defense attorney could take note of this in order to bring you into a bad light.

The sentence above could be reworded to say, "I hit him in the stomach and then threw him down."

6 Use of Excessive Force

A person who uses excessive force when he fears for his life or is in a deadly fright is generally not held liable. The law is generally along these lines but varies in different countries and you should check on the applicable law, as the subject is often controversial. If, according to your statements, it is clear that you could defend yourself without any problem, and even felt good doing so, but that you used excessive force, then you can be made liable in certain circumstances.

Example:

An attacker, A, punches your head. You block the punch with your lower arm and throw A down to the ground. As a result A is knocked unconscious. You are so upset over the attack that you then kick A in the face. The kick was unnecessary and constitutes the use of excessive force.

However, if you were afraid for your life, the situation could be formulated as follows:
"A threw a punch at my head. I don't know what I did then. Out of fear for my life I thrashed about and kicked out. A then, somehow or other, fell down and I don't know how this happened." In such a case it could well be that you would then not be held liable for the use of excessive force.

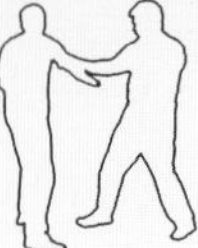

Later in this book you will find suggestions for effective combinations. If you use one of these and the attacker is rendered incapable during its execution, then I recommend that you consider not using any further techniques as these could be construed as the use of excessive force.

It is quite understandable that you could overreact out of fear of a further attack – perhaps a more brutal one. However this won't help in a court of law.

7 Excusing Yourself

As a basic premise in a lawsuit, it is advantageous when witnesses to the event have gained the impression that you regret your reactions to the attack. It is therefore recommended that you express this by saying sorry several times. Because the witnesses may be some distance away at the time and may not overhear what is said, it is a good thing to use body language – perhaps like this:

Lay both of your hands on your cheeks as if you wanted to say, "What have I done?"

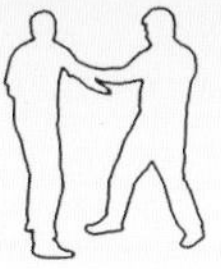

8 Am I Allowed to Carry a Weapon?

At this juncture, I advise you against carrying a knife or a gas pistol. If you have a knife with you and you are attacked and use it to defend yourself, then there is the danger that this will be construed as criminal intent. What are you going to say when questioned? Perhaps, you'll say that you carry the knife around so that you can peel fruit? If you must carry an aid with you, then I recommend a tear gas spray or pepper foam.

9 Aids That You Can Buy to Protect Yourself

I'm always being asked in my classes if there isn't some form of aid or weapon that you can use to defend yourself with. Of course there are aids such as tear gas, electric shock batons, hand sirens, piercing whistle alarms and gas pistols. However, check first with your local police office whether you are allowed to carry any of these items e.g., to a concert or similar event. As a general rule all of the items mentioned are not allowed.

If you carry any of the items with you, you must always be ready for the attacker to wrest the item off you and use it against you.

Think about the following points:

- The defender can become reliant on the instrument and neglect the basic techniques.
- Going around carrying the aid is not often practiced and tested.
- The aid must be handy. If there is an emergency, it is too late to start fumbling in the pocket of your pants for it.
- Gas sprays have to be around the size of deodorant spray bottle otherwise their use is questionable due to the limited spray range possible. Used in a room or against the wind, the gas can harm you or bystanders. If the bystanders are harmed, they could sue you for bodily harm. In particular a pepper spray is in such cases very dangerous and normally may not be used

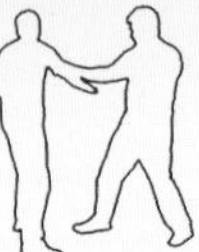

against people. In an emergency situation you are only allowed to injure the attacker and not those innocent onlookers. You could also use a colored spray paint can. This will make it easy for the police to recognize the culprit.

- When using hand sirens or piercing whistle alarms, an innocent bystander does not have to assume you are in danger of being attacked. The piercing whistle can be used against telephone harassment. You should note though that using this method can cause the culprit to suffer a ruptured eardrum.

- A baton, with or without an electric shock facility, is about 30 cm long. Its length alone makes its use questionable. Telescopic ones are also usable, but here again it takes time to extend it before using it.

- Most people will have some form of inhibition about firing off a gas pistol. If this is done under 1m away from the attacker, there is the danger that he can be blinded or have serious burns caused to his face.

- From a distance it is not easily clear which the defender is and which person the attacker is. Gas pistols also resemble a real pistol. The police can easily misinterpret the situation when they see one of them holding a pistol pointed at someone else and assume that that person holding the pistol is the attacker.

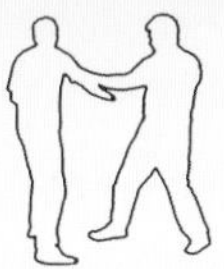

10 Using a Pepper Spray or Pepper Foam

Pepper sprays may not be used against people. It is a very effective item, because it causes the eye reflex to close the eyes even in people under the influence of drugs and also dogs. Using other types of sprays doesn't always have the same effect. When jogging, you have a pepper spray with you because you have a great fear of dogs (you have the spray only for this reason!) and suddenly you are attacked by a man – then you can use the spray against him to defend yourself. However, if the spray affects other people around, then you can expect to be sued for bodily harm by them. Recently, in a beer tent, a woman successfully used a pepper spray against her friend (who wanted to beat her up). 30 people around her, however, were injured as a result – some even requiring treatment in a clinic. The compensation for injuries sustained will be considerable – so think very carefully before you use this very effective aid. By the way, this applies to any of the other aids. If innocent bystanders are injured, then you can expect to be sued for damages.

11 What Happens in Your Body When Being Attacked?

When you suddenly get into a fearful panic, the body produces adrenalin and noradrenalin. These have the effect that further elements are produced in the brain that cause the digestive system to shut down and you feel a funny, queasy feeling in the stomach. Your blood pressure increases, the hands become sweaty and some people become incontinent. In this panic the brain blocks and you get a sort of tunnel vision. On top of this, the body in such a situation is not quite so sensitive to pain (and this is an advantage).

Under normal conditions you are able to call on about 60% of your strength – if you are a fit person this will be about 70-80% – the remainder of your strength is required for breathing, circulation and emergencies and you can do nothing about these things.

When having to defend yourself (in a state of shock) these reserves are released. You are now capable of things that you would never have dreamed of. If you do something to defend yourself e.g., you head butt the attacker, you will have considerably more energy behind it than if you were not in such a fearful panic.

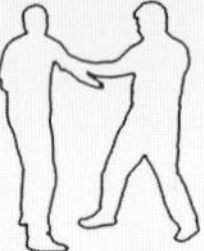

Sometimes people who have had an accident and are in a state of shock experience this situation. It is not without reason that in a First Aid course you learn to sit a shock patient down and calm him down by talking to him and telling him that he is OK.

Once in a competition, I received several hits in the face. Of course I knew that this had happened but I had no pain. It wasn't until after the fight on the way to take a shower that my jaw began to ache. It was so sore that I could only manage to eat soup that evening.

You can also often read about people who have been stabbed several times, but have managed to keep up their defense successfully and only realized later that they were wounded. During the defense they put up they hadn't felt a thing.

12 Are You Being Followed?

If you have a feeling that you are being followed then turn around. This is advantageous for the following reasons:

- It is easier to defend yourself facing the attacker than trying to ward off an attack from behind.
- You can see who is behind you. Perhaps it is only a small child who is running after you.
- Speak to the person following you directly where there are other people around who can help you if needed. If you wait too long, then the attack can take place where there is nobody to help you.

13 Speak Directly to People Who You Ask to Help

Don't simply call out, "Help! Help me please!" because many people will not feel that they are the ones meant. They would be afraid of also becoming a victim. If you want help, speak to the person directly.

Example:

"Hello, you there with the green shirt, please help me!"

14 Call on People Standing Around to Help You When Another Person is Being Attacked

If you want to help a person who is being threatened, but are anxious about doing it alone then speak to other people standing around so that you can get them to help collectively. They often see the wrongdoing, but don't have the courage to offer to help. With two or three of you, the situation looks quite different. It is often the case that women have more courage than men in such situations and help without being asked.

15 Remain Formal

Don't be tempted to try to mollify the situation in the way you speak to the attacker – this never really pays off.

16 'No!' Means 'No!'

Has it ever happened to you that, for example, you ask a colleague or a friend whether he would come with you for a coffee? Maybe he answered, "No!" Did you accept his "No!" ? Probably not. You then persisted with, "Oh come on, let's go for a coffee." Even then you didn't let him off the hook and you kept on at him until he gave in and went with you, or, in a loud voice he said, "STOP IT NOW! I'M NOT COMING! JUST ACCEPT THAT NOW." This was the "No!" that you probably had to accept in the end.

Make sure when you are in a dangerous situation that "No!" means just that – "NO!"

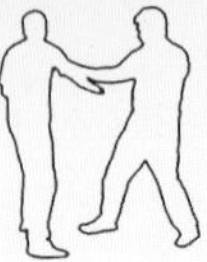

17 You Say 'NO!' but Your Body Indicates 'YES!'

Referring back to the example with the coffee. It is often the case that when someone gives a final 'No' they also give a little laugh. The listener hearing this will get about 10% meaning from this but about 50% meaning from the body language. This explains why we often don't take the first 'No' from someone, because his body is saying something else. You can test this well on babies. Say something negative and laugh as you say this. The baby will probably laugh back at you. Vice versa, if you say something positive and put on an aggressive face together with your voice then the baby will probably cry.

Back up what you say with an appropriate body language:

- Look displeased
- Look the person up and down
- Square your shoulders
- Puff up your chest and make yourself tall
- Bring your hands up so that you can keep the other person at a distance
- Say out loud and in a determined voice – "NO!"

This attitude is not only important in self-defense. It can also serve you well in everyday life.

18 How Close Should You Allow a Person to Get Near You?

Dependent on how big you are, we find it unpleasant when someone gets too near you. Let's test this out. Get a stranger to run at you and say, "STOP" when it gets uncomfortable. The distance will be about a 2 m radius around you.

Someone you know can come within this radius, but even then you would want him to be about one arms length away from you.

In closer situations or circles where another person can be close to you, only let your children or your friend enter this area.

19 'STOP!' Means Just That - 'STOP!'

If a person gets too near to you, make sure he clearly understands that he is getting too close to you for your comfort. I have made it a habit that I bring my arms forward and 'let them do the talking.' In cases where strangers are involved, give a clear "STOP!" As you say this, square your shoulders and stand up tall, look at him deliberately and hold your arms forward in front of your body. If the stranger disregards this command, then you should be prepared to have to use one of the techniques described in this book.

20 Surprise the Attacker

Our bodies react to different stimuli, and categorize these into 'dangerous' or 'not dangerous'. Perhaps you have experienced turning around and being surprised by someone standing close behind you. Your body reacts to the visual stimulus. It could be that you didn't see the person, and you become aware of him first when he, for example, touches you. This we call reaction to a physical stimulus. Alternatively it could be that you become aware of him as the person suddenly says something. You are then reacting to an acoustic stimulus.

Just imagine, you think you are alone in your apartment when suddenly your husband/friend or acquaintance jumps towards you and grabs both of your upper

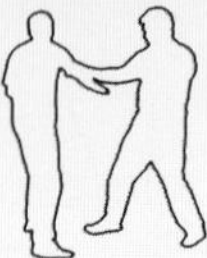

arms, shakes you and shouts into your face. You will be probably terribly frightened and for a short while (transistory vagotonic shock phase) unable to move. According to the severity of the shock, this length of time can be very different lasting anything between a half and 20 seconds. When going on the defensive you should always try to shock your attacker. When he is in a state of shock, his reflexes and body functions are disrupted and you are more easily able to use your defense techniques. You stand the best chance of success by using all three stimuli together:

- Visual
- Physical
- Acoustic

Below is a list of suggested ways at achieving a shock effect:

- Shouting loudly
- Spitting into the face
- Biting
- Puffing your chest and standing tall
- Spraying tear gas, hairspray or car paint spray into the face
- Throwing an object (e.g., a key or a newspaper) into the face
- Delivering a punch or kick
- Calling for an imaginary person ("Hey, Bob – Help me!")
- Calling for an imaginary dog ("Here, boy – grab him!")

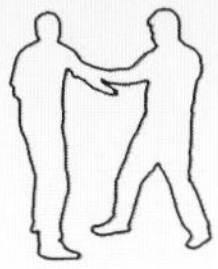

21 How You Should Act in a Defensive Situation

In this section is a list of some suggestions on how you should act in a defensive situation. If you use them in such a case, you will have a better chance of successfully defending yourself.

- Concentrate on your breathing. Try to breathe calmly to reduce your nervousness.
- If you expect an attack from behind, turn around to face the attacker. An attack from behind places you at a disadvantage.
- If help is close by, then run away from the attack shouting out loud.
- If help is not close by then stand your ground and face the attacker. If you are a woman then you have particularly good chances that when you start to defend yourself the attacker breaks off – according to statistics 9 out of 10 attacks end like this.
- Don't lose sight of the attacker. Watch the whole of his body. If you only look at his eyes, you will realize too late that he is about to use his legs.
- Adopt your personal defensive stance lifting your arms to cover yourself so that your actions are unmistakable to the attacker. Try to gain some distance away from the attacker. Various "neutral defensive stances" are described further on in this book.
- Try to get an obstacle between you and the attacker so that you can gain time when attacked. This is of even greater importance if the attacker has a weapon.
- Anybody in a radius of 6 m around you can pose a potential threat to you. Various studies have shown that an injury from a distance of 6 m (when the attacker storms at you) is almost unavoidable. Bystanders could also be party to the attacker – so – be on the lookout.
- Don't bend down to pick up a weapon. If you have managed to disarm an attacker, position yourself over it and push/pull it away with you until you are at least 6 m away from any other person present. Then you can pick it up. An acquaintance of the attacker could use your bending down to their own good and kick you, for example, in the face as you bend to pick it up.

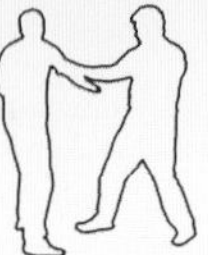

22 You Come Across a Fistfight

Running away is not cowardly – it is rather clever. Cross over the road or circumvent the incident as far as this is possible. This way you keep out of danger.

23 Go Around in Pairs

If you're out together with another person and you have the impression that an attack on you could take place, you should have already agreed with the other whether you are both going to run away or stay and fight. Otherwise it could happen that one of you runs away and the other is left to stay and fight. You should always be on the lookout, checking as you go. If you are deep in conversation, you could overlook or spot someone who is approaching you too late. In such a case, as described earlier, the shock phase could be longer.

24 Defense Against More Than One Attacker

Facing one attacker is bad enough, but what can you do when there are more of them?

- Don't stand between them. In such a position, you will rarely get away without being injured. Position yourself so that one of the attackers is in front of the other thus allowing only one at a time the opportunity to attack you.

- Your reaction against the first attacker must be carried out hard enough so that he is not in a position to attack you again in the next few minutes. There are combinations in this book that can be used to eliminate the attacker.

- If you are being held by more than one attacker, consider the following:

  > Never try to free a hold with force. You must assume that the attacker is stronger than you – save your strength for something more effective.

Consider which of your extremities is free (including your head). If you have a hand free you could, for example, jab him in the eyes, break his nose or chop into his neck (larynx) (take care here as this is life threatening). If you manage to achieve any of these, there is a good chance he will stop. If your leg is free, you could knee him in the genitals, kick out at his knee, rub the outside of your shoe down his shin or stamp on his foot. These techniques won't misfire either.

25 When Fighting Back Is Not a Possibility

The attacker is holding a knife to your throat or is standing a few meters away holding a firearm. If you are ever in such a situation, first of all don't try to use any self-defense techniques, but rather talk to the person quietly. As long as the attacker is only demanding money, jewelry, purse or a piece of your clothing (e.g., your coat), then hand them over. If he wants to rape you, try to delude him into thinking you will go along with his demands. Tell him that you want to go into the bedroom, because perhaps the children will come home. Wait until he has put the weapon down before you attempt to use a self-defense technique (as described later in this book).

26 The Expensive Car With the Electronic Anti-Theft Device

Most new cars are equipped with a fail-safe electronic anti-theft device. These devices are so good that many car thieves, as professional as some are, don't risk disarming it for fear of the time it takes during which they could be caught in the act. The thief operates, nowadays, by watching and following the owner. When he then knows where the owner lives, he waits until dark, breaks in and steals the vehicle keys. Getting through the main door is the least of his problems. Some owners keep the keys under their pillow and this is dangerous. Better to leave the keys in a key safe. The vehicle is likely, more than probably, to be insured against theft so little could happen to you personally.

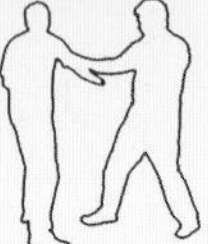

27 How to Defend Yourself in Various Places

27.1 In the elevator

Few people will have given a thought as to whether it makes sense to stand on any particular spot or corner when in an elevator. If you are attacked in an elevator, the choosing the right spot can help to avoid the worst. If you are on your own, you should stand near the operating panel. The advantage of this is that if someone gets in you don't like the look of, then you can easily press the button for the next floor where you get out. You can also press the alarm button. If the attacker is standing by the panel then he can send the elevator down to the basement or up to the roof and this could spell trouble for you.

27.2 In the parking lot

Parking lot owners don't like it if you reverse in to a slot to park, because of the emissions damage or dirt on the wall. However, it is considerably safer to park in backwards rather than forwards. Why? When you park in forwards then all you see is the wall. What don't you see – well yes – is the rest of the parking lot. An attacker

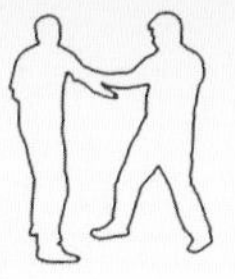

could creep up on you from behind the vehicle, rip open the door and grab you. If you park in backwards, you can see the whole parking lot in front of you. If an attacker then tries to open the door you could put your foot down on the gas pedal and drive away. While the attacker could keep hold of the door, after a short time he would be forced to let go. Of course this might cause damage to the bodywork but at least this can be easily repaired.

27.3 In the subway

If, at night, you are in the subway, don't get into an empty compartment. If the train is completely empty, sit in the compartment directly behind the driver. There is bound to be an emergency brake somewhere near this spot. If an attack occurs, you are within easy reach of the emergency brake.

27.4 In the car

27.4.1 The attacker is sitting behind you

When driving straight forwards and the attacker harasses you from the rear passenger seat, it is more than likely that he has not fastened his seatbelt. Take hold of the steering wheel at 12 o'clock as if you were looking at your watch and, dependent on the traffic about, turn the wheel sharply to the left (in UK – the right) and carry out an emergency stop. This will cause the attacker to be thrown to the right. Unclip your seatbelt with the right hand and as soon as the vehicle comes to a halt and leave the vehicle as fast as you can.

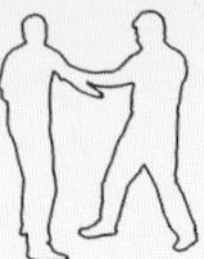

27.4.2 The attacker is sitting next to you

Again, I must emphasize that I assume that you are being confronted by a seriously dangerous attack e.g., an imminent rape and that you are not as strong as the attacker. This is the reason behind suggesting such a fierce reaction to the attack. It would still be better if you could solve the conflict verbally.

As you do an emergency stop (providing traffic allows this), deliver a backhand strike at the attacker's nose or a knife edge strike at his larynx (careful – life threatening) and then undo your seatbelt with the right hand (UK – left hand) and get out of the vehicle. If you are sitting next to the driver, wait until the vehicle has almost come to a stop and then deliver one of the strike techniques mentioned. You can undo the seatbelt just before you do this.

If the vehicle is stopped and the attacker molests you, then you should react as follows:

1. Don't try first of all to free yourself from the grip, irrespective where he is holding you (e.g., in a stranglehold or, in the case of women, by the breasts or between the legs).

2. Think which extremity of your body is still free (including your head).

If your head is free then do a head butt on the attacker. If you are a woman and the attacker is kissing you then try to hold him firmly so that he cannot free himself and then bite him hard. Keep biting him. One bite can cause pain - several create panic. Because you are holding the attacker firmly, he cannot get away and the bites are something quite worrying for him.

I once read in a newspaper that a policeman was bitten like this and as a result he was four weeks off work. Four weeks is a long time, so the bites must have been rather hefty. If your hand is free, you can use a finger jab to the eyes, break his nose or do a hand chop at his larynx (careful – life threatening). If you have a good chance of hitting him in the genitals then you could do this also.

28 Telephone Harassment

Some people are terrorized by another, who rings up pestering on the telephone day and night. If the person isn't threatening but says something like "I love you, I love you" then you have virtually no rapid chance of catching them. In such cases you can use an answering machine and let the caller talk to his heart's desire. Only when the calls go on for a long time, and you can get a doctor's note explaining that this is putting you in a nervous disposition, can you get a trace and obtain an official complaint against the person to stop him from calling you.

One means that is very effective in these cases is a shrill whistle. When the call comes again you can blow the whistle loudly on the phone. You must realize, however, that this can rupture the attacker's eardrum. Therefore, make sure you take the handset away from your own ear so that you don't injure yourself by the echo.

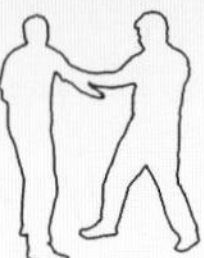

29 Train Yourself to Be Able to Describe People

Train yourself to be able to describe other people. Just take a quick look at somebody and then try to remember as many details as you can. You will realize just how difficult this is. When trying to defend yourself, being under stress, you will find it even more difficult to remember things afterwards.

Possible questions:

- How tall was the person?
- How old was the person?
- What color eyes did the person have?
- What did his nose, mouth and ears look like?
- Did the person have a full beard, a goatee or a moustache?
- Did the person have any distinguishing features (scars, tattoos, piercings, birthmarks or moles, etc.)?
- How did the person speak (language, dialect, stuttering, etc.)?
- How did the person speak (vulgarly, aggressively, normally, etc.)?
- Did the person have a deformity (limp, finger missing, etc.)?
- What was the person wearing (cap, coat, pants, etc.)?
- Were there any distinguishing marks on the clothing (dirt, badges, etc.)?
- Did the person have a weapon (knife, stick, pistol, etc.)?

......and so on and so forth.

30 Defense Against Dog Attacks

30.1 Self-defense against a dog attack

During many years as a follower of martial arts, now and again I have experienced how to defend against dogs in several various courses. This was quite fun because one of the students acted as the dog. However, if a large dog is standing in front of your baring its teeth, I am not so sure that you would want to strike out with your arms and legs because the dog would easily be able to bite into them. So – what can you do?

- If a dog runs up to you, never try to run away, because this could stir up its hunting instinct and it will follow you and perhaps bite you.
- If the dog doesn't stop within 5 m of you, you can try shouting at it – this occasionally helps.
- If the dog stops and starts barking at you, don't run away at any cost. I can't say whether it is better to stare the animal out or not, because it depends on the dog. For example, if you have one of the so-called 'dangerous' dogs in front of you, it could be that the animal will interpret your look as a challenge and attack you. If it is not one of the dangerous categorized animals, it will probably back off if you outstare it. If you have been a dog owner then you will know how to judge what sort is confronting you. If the owner of the dog is in the neighborhood, then wait until they come and put the dog on the lead. Otherwise, make a big circle around the dog to get by.
- If the dog does not react to your shouting and jumps up at you, you can give it a solid punch in the chest. This makes many dogs break off, because they are very sensitive in this region.
- If you have sufficient time before the attack and you have a coat or a pullover in your hand, you can wrap this around your arm and use it to defend yourself (i.e., offering it for the dog to grab hold of).
- If you know your way around the martial arts, it is quite possible for you to use one of the sweeping techniques to knock away a dog jumping up at you. Of course, it is then possible that a further attack will take place, and you must use one of the other techniques described.

- If the dog has got your hand in his teeth and is biting, then push your hand further down its throat as far as possible until it gags and lets go of your hand. This won't be easy to do, but is, nevertheless, one way of surviving a dog attack.

1

2

- If the dog is biting your lower arm, with your free hand you can press into the dog's chaps (fleshy lip part of the dog's mouth) and open its mouth. With the open hand come down over the ridge of the dog's nose and press down on the lips against its teeth with the thumb on the one side and the fingers on the other side. If the dog now tries to bite, it will bite its own lips (which will hurt him). Dog owners know about this kind of grip, but it will be a bit strange for the uninitiated. I am quite aware that the uninitiated will need lots of will power to do this, but it is good chance that you will be freed from the dog's grip this way. It would be quite wrong to pull your arm away until the dog has let go as this could cause greater injuries by ripping open the wound.

1

2

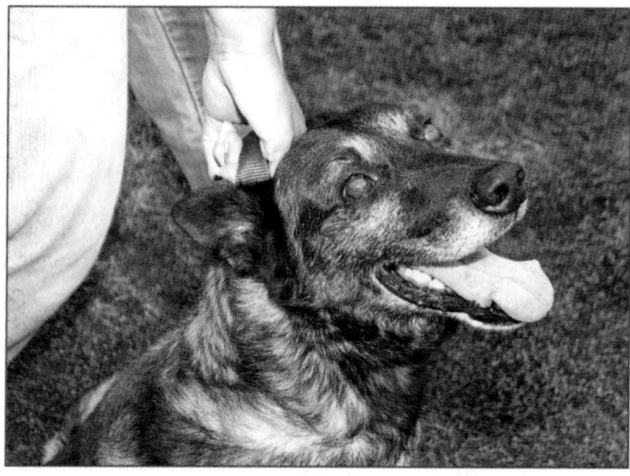

- If the dog has a collar on and is biting you, get hold of the collar with your free hand and twist it. Within a few seconds the dog will not be able to breathe and it will let you arm go. Keep on using the stranglehold and pull the dog up into the air and away from you in order to increase the strangling effect. Let go when someone (e.g., the dog owner) takes the dog off you.

- Further sensitive points on the dog are its eyes, nose, ears and genitals (male dogs). You can use the following techniques:

- Finger jab to the eyes.

- Smack on the nose.

- Grab hold of the ears and pull them hard.

- Kick it in the genitals.

- Do a knife-hand chop against its throat **(this could kill the dog!)**.

Remember, however, that all these techniques could make the dog more aggressive.

- With fighting dogs, particularly pitbulls, the techniques suggested above are questionable, because this type of dog is insensitive to the measures. Even a kick in the genitals may not have any effect. With this type, the only way is the strangling method using the collar.

- If you have a pepper spray or foam with you, you could use this. Take care, however, that nobody standing around gets injured from this as well, otherwise you can expect to be sued. The pepper spray is a very effective method against dogs because the eyes react by shutting.

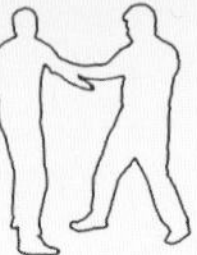

30.2 Stopping a dog attack

You come across a situation where a dog is biting someone else or has bitten someone. You can reckon on being bitten yourself if you try to intervene. It is therefore clear to me that you have to summon up courage to do so. If you decide to wade in, then you must do this resolutely. You can undertake the following:

- Grab hold of the dog's collar, twist it and pull so that you cause a strangling reaction. The dog will soon let go of its grip. Don't let go of the collar until someone else has taken the dog off you otherwise you won't have any further control over it.

- Grab hold of the dog at the rear in its groins and lift its back part up so that its head is hanging down and it cannot bite any more.

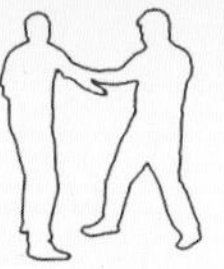

31 Vital Nerve Points (Attack Points) on the Body and Possible Injuries

In the following section, the different vital nerve points on the body are described. The resulting injuries are also described if these points are attacked.

31.1 Head

- Eyes (loss of sight)
- Nose (broken)
- Ears (loss of hearing/ unconsciousness)
- Temples (unconsciousness)
- Chin (unconsciousness)
- Cheekbone (broken)

Depending on how hard the head has been hit (e.g., with a head butt) there is a danger of concussion or even a fractured skull.

If you cause an injury to one of these vital points on the attacker's head, you must assume that he will be severely injured. Remember that the defense must be relative to the attack. If this is not the case you can reckon on being sued for causing bodily harm. This carries a punishment of different lengths of jailtime, dependent upon where you live. The verbal solution to a conflict is always the preferred one.

31.2 Neck

- Larynx **(Danger of death! If the larynx is damaged badly, a tracheotomy must be performed to save the life)**.
- Sinus nodes (can cause death by disruption of the cardiac rhythm).
- Carotid artery (unconsciousness).

31.3 Collar bone (breaks)

31.4 Chest

- Right half of the chest (breathing problems and circulatory problems).
- Left half of the chest (breathing problems and circulatory problems).
- Solar plexus (unconsciousness).
- Liver (unconsciousness, breathing problems, damaged/ripped).
- Spleen (unconsciousness, damaged/ripped).

31.5 Back

- Spine (damaged vertebrae, paralysis, slipped disc).
- Kidneys (urinating blood, damaged, unconsciousness).

31.6 Arms

- Shoulder joint (broken and/or restricted movement of the arms).
- Elbow joint (broken and/or restricted movement of the arms).
- Wrist joint (broken and/or restricted movement of the arms and hands).
- Hand joint (broken and/or restricted movement of the arms and hands).

31.7 Genitals (Impotence, Unconsciousness)

31.8 Legs

- Hip joint (restricted movement of the hips).
- Knee joint (damaged knee and/or restricted movement of the leg).
- Shin (broken shin and/or restricted movement of the leg).
- Foot (broken and/or restricted movement of the leg).

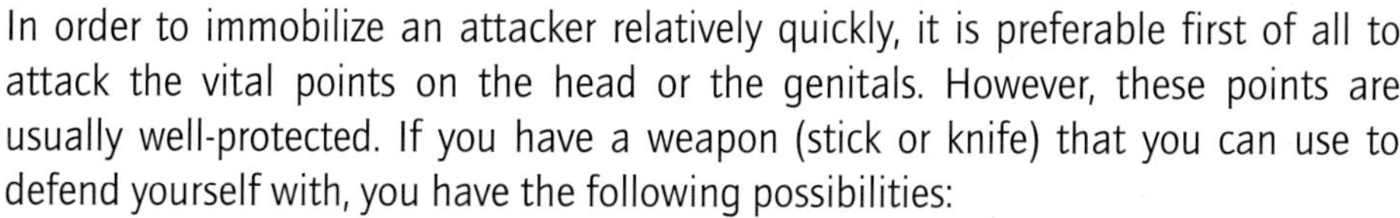

In order to immobilize an attacker relatively quickly, it is preferable first of all to attack the vital points on the head or the genitals. However, these points are usually well-protected. If you have a weapon (stick or knife) that you can use to defend yourself with, you have the following possibilities:

An inexperienced attacker will not concentrate so much on his left hand; therefore a strike or jab at that hand can be very successful. When the attacker's hand is hurting, you can carry out other attacks, for example, at his right hand (i.e., the one holding the weapon) or against his head.

If you don't have a weapon, you can use a diversionary maneuver; for example, kick out at his legs before you attack the arms or the head.

However, always remember that the defense technique must be relative to the fierceness of the attack.

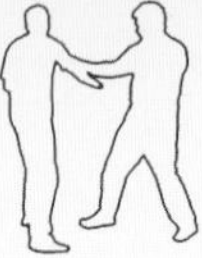

32 Defense Techniques

32.1 Techniques using the hands

Hand techniques include:

- Punches (particularly a series of punches, one after the other).

- Punches (strikes with the back of the hand, swinging punches, uppercuts, hammer blows with the fist).

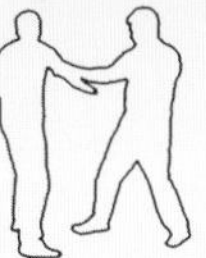

- Knife-hand strikes.

- Finger and hand jabs.

- Strikes and slaps with the palm of the hand.

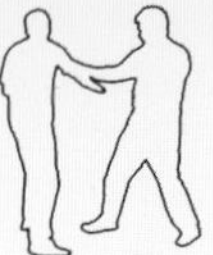

You should try to deliver your punches using full concentration, strength and speed and take the shortest route to the target. As your punch lands on the attacker's body, it will have the maximum energy. The effect is increased by hitting the target with the smallest possible striking surface. For women, the finger jab and open palm strikes are particularly suitable, because many of them clench their fists incorrectly and they can even break the hand by hitting with a bent wrist.

- Knife-hand attacks are targeted against the larynx, temples, carotid artery, nose or at the genitals.
- Finger jabs can be done using one, two or five fingers. Targets are the eyes and the genitals. For the latter, use of all five fingers is recommended as it is more likely to land on the target (in case the attacker moves).
- The palm strikes are primarily best used against the nose and the larynx.

All these techniques can cause serious injury to the attacker and even in some cases prove fatal.

32.2 Kicks and 'punches' using the feet

These include:

- A kick forwards, sideways, to the rear and upwards.
- A foot 'punch' forwards and to the rear.

These techniques can be used by the practiced martial arts follower:

- Roundhouse kick forwards and backwards.
- Low kick at the shin.
- Stamping kick.

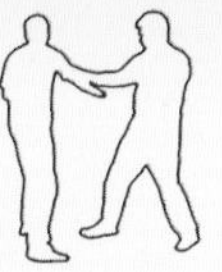

1 stamping punch forward with foot

2 stamping punch upwards with foot

3 sideways

4 backwards

The difference between a kick and foot 'punch' is that a kick is executed with help of the hip pushing the leg forward, while a foot 'punch' is a straight stamping movement. Without any previous training, it will be difficult to carry out kicks and foot punches above the belt. Targets below the belt are the attacker's genitals, the knees, the shins and the instep of the foot.

The kick forwards, and the sideways and upwards stamping 'punch' with the foot are the most effective ones. The kick forwards is generally used to attack the genitals, because, when successful, the attacker rarely counters. We then have kicks used against the knees and shins. Both possibilities can cause a lot of pain. If a kick carried out at the knee is done with a lot of force, there is a danger that the leg could be broken.

There are two ways of carrying out the 'punching' kick. One is to tuck the toes in so that the striking surface is the ball of the foot. The second way – with the back of the foot – is particularly suitable for use in kicking the genitals. In both methods, the knee is lifted up and then with a snap movement of the leg and foot, the kick is delivered. A kick with the toes stretched out forwards can be very painful for the defender.

The sideways 'punching' kick is good for use against the knees. Your own knee is first of all lifted up and then the leg is 'punched' down against the attacker's knee or against the hollow at the back of his knee.

The 'punching' kick backwards is particularly suitable if you are being held in a bear hug.

roundhouse kick forwards

roundhouse kick backwards

shin kick

It is directed at the attacker's instep. The knee is lifted up rapidly and the foot is brought down stamping on the attacker's foot.

It will also be painful if, when doing a shin kick, you scrape the sole of your foot down the shin thus grazing the skin.

32.3 Strikes and thrusts using the elbow

Strikes and thrusts using the elbow include:

- Striking with the elbow forwards, to the rear and upwards.
- Thrusting with the elbow sideways, to the rear and downwards.

The difference between a strike and a thrust with the elbow is that the strike is done straight while the thrust is brought around in a semi-circle. Ideally, the striking surface is the point of the elbow. However, striking the target with the lower arm is also sufficient. Techniques using the elbow are particularly suitable for the untrained person, because they can be done with force and, unlike in a punch, there is no danger that the hand can be broken.

Strikes using the elbow can also be targeted against the attacker's striking hand. In the worst case the attacker's hand can get broken in such cases.

1 Elbow strike forwards

2 Elbow strike upwards

3 Elbow strike to the rear

1 Elbow thrust to the rear

2 Elbow thrust upwards

3 Elbow thrust to the rear

4 Elbow thrust sideways

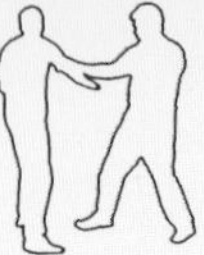

32.4 Strikes and thrusts using the knee

The main difference between these two techniques is that for the thrust using the knee, the leg is lifted up and the knee is thrust forwards with a hip movement. In the strike using the knee, the knee is brought upwards in a semi-circular motion. Knee strikes are especially recommended for the untrained person as they can be easily learned and, like elbow strikes, achieve a good effect with relatively little effort.

You should use the knee against the genital area, but remember the dangers of causing injury. Knees are one of the hardest 'body weapons.'

32.5 Throws and lever techniques

Throws and lever techniques can be effective ones, but they have a big disadvantage. They must be regularly practiced and trained longer than punching and kicking techniques. Besides this, during training, the thrown party has to master the fall techniques if he is not to be injured. The principle of the throwing techniques is to cause the person to be thrown to lose his balance through a pulling or pushing action and not give him any chance of having something to support himself with. Providing you are physically superior to the opponent, these techniques can be used very successfully.

In a lever technique, the aim is to bring pressure against the natural movement of the joints or the way they operate by stretching or twisting them.

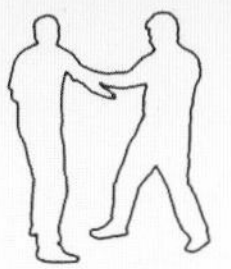

33 Attacks by Males Against Males

In the following section, two types of fighter are described.

33.1 Gunslingers

The gunslinger visits the bar on weekends in order to pick a fight with another. He deliberately targets his victim and provokes him until there is a fight. The gunslinger often surprises his victim with an attack. He stands next to the victim, turns to one side, lays, for example, his drink down and turns back towards the victim and suddenly attacks him without warning. So – be careful when a stranger comes up to the bar alongside you. Watch his movements and be prepared for a surprise attack. I have included a few combinations in this book for the particular situation when you are in a bar.

A typical pose for the gunslinger is making eye contact with his victim – usually someone who doesn't look away. If they stare at each other then the next phase starts. Elephants flap their ears, trumpet and start a charge. Elephant seals lift up their torsos, bellow and crawl rapidly towards the invader. One finds many more examples like these in the animal world. The gunslinger acts similarly. His voice gets louder; he squares his shoulders, lifts his eyebrows and begins to make threatening gestures.

If you are not keen on such an incident, then don't hold your eye contact longer than necessary. Never drop your gaze as this means weakness. A fight between two men usually starts with them both holding each other's eye contact. This is the same with animals. In Chapter 30, "Defense against dog attacks", you can find more points. Many men feel the urge to avoid being classed as a 'weakling' and this leads to them holding eye contact too long, often ending in a fight. The next phase then begins – pushing and shoving – just like animals do.

Recently, however, I witnessed a surprise fight without any 'foreplay' with the attacker delivering a straight uppercut at the victim's chin. The victim was hit so hard he could not react and the attacker had an easy prey. Further on in this book, I have included 'neutral' defense postures that you can surely use in such a case.

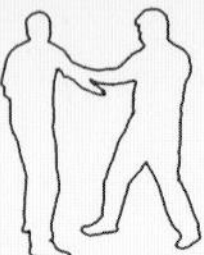

33.2 Cat and mouse

The big, bold cat is always out to get its prey – the little gray mouse. He mainly hunts at night during the weekends, combing the bars and discos looking for a target physically inferior to him. He searches out his prey seemingly carefully to make sure he isn't taking on something he cannot handle. He takes note whether the person could be dangerous for him. Is his potential victim fit with muscles? Does he have a boxer's nose? – Here he could expect a vigorous defender. What picture does his victim present? Is he a strapping lad or does he sit there like a sack? Then he finds what he is looking for – perhaps, the fat, unsporting type with rimmed glasses – and that's his target.

The incident usually takes the following form:

1. Eye contact.
2. Verbal lead-up.
3. Pushing and shoving.
4. The first blows.

1. Eye contact

The big, bold cat has done his reconnaissance and made eye contact. The gray mouse (victim) feels something unpleasant in the air, but cannot make it out exactly. He is standing there with the rest and looks the big, bold cat in the face. He quickly diverts his glance because he has the feeling, he doesn't like what he sees. Our little, gray mouse now makes a dramatic mistake and looks down at the ground. This shows clearly that he is inferior to the big, bold cat and the sequence now begins to roll out.

2. Verbal lead-up and closing the distance

Unfortunately, the short eye contact has spurred the big, bold cat to leave his spot and advance on the little, gray mouse. Then come the words tumbling out – "Want something? Why are you looking at me then?" or "Do you want me? Then why are you looking at me like that?" The little, gray mouse is totally beside himself, shrinks away, looks the other way and hopes that the everything will just pass by.

3. Closing the distance, body contact and pushing and shoving

Sorry – but it doesn't go away! The cat pushes the mouse or grabs the lapels of his coat and then the cat hammers out further slants, for example, "And now, you little mouse, you messing your pants? Eh!" He could be right! If there's no counter to this move, then the big, bold cat gets bigger and the little, gray mouse gets smaller.

4. The first blows

By now the situation has grown so that the little, gray mouse has collapsed into himself from fear and the big, bold cat is standing over him with his chest puffed out. Now come the first blows and the crushing attack. The little, gray mouse is standing there completely in shock and not in any way able to react to defend himself and subsequently gets a severe beating up.

B ATTACKS AGAINST WOMEN

1 Has a Woman Any Chance Against an Attacking Male?

I get this question at least once in every course I run. I would like to impart to you my experience on this subject.

I had a few competition fights already behind me and had won more than several times. Then, one day I entered another competition. My opponent held an orange belt. You can gain this belt after about one year's training. At that time I held a 2nd black belt. So – what happened? As usual, I stepped up onto the mat, calling to my mates, "See you in a minute!" After all, it shouldn't be a problem to be able to beat a "beginner" quickly.

The judge called out, "Fight!" and I ran towards my opponent quite relaxed. My opponent then got hold of me, lifted me up and threw me in a matter of seconds down onto the mat. I was so surprised that I wasn't in a position to be able to reclaim my lost points. After the fight, I learned that my opponent held a 2nd black belt in a different martial arts discipline (Judo in this case). If I hadn't been so self-assured and taken my opponent seriously, then I would have perhaps saved myself this defeat.

What I want to say here is that a man doesn't attack a woman while holding his hands in front of his genitals or his eyes. Men feel themselves to be superior to women. After all they are "MEN." In this aura of absolute high-handedness, men don't particularly think there will be any reaction from a woman – they're easy prey, so to speak. Maybe they think that there will be a little scuffle, but not that they can have their eyes plucked out, their nose broken, the larynx smashed or their genitals, knees or shins damaged.

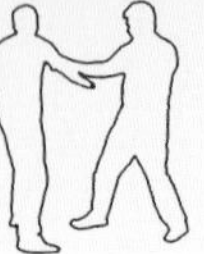

If you stand there with your body posture exuding self-assurance (i.e., shoulders squared, eyebrows raised and eyes wide open, etc.) this will signal, "Oh no! Not with me!" This alone will put off many a man wanting to attack you. Your resistance begins in your mind. If you decide to defend yourself and react forcefully, rapidly and determinedly, then in all probability you will succeed.

In my generation, we were brought up that girls should not get dirty. They always had to be well-behaved and shouldn't scream. Fighting and brawling were reserved for the boys. Again and again, I have learned in my seminars that there are many women who simply cannot scream and we have to work hard at it to get them to be able to do so. Lots of women also believe that they aren't strong enough to defend themselves and that they can't bring themselves to hurt someone. Others have been so brainwashed by their husbands/friends and so negatively motivated to think that they "don't have a chance – let it be!" As I said before, "Resistance begins in the mind." If you are going to want to defend yourself seriously, then you must first make up your mind to learn the necessary techniques, either on your own, or better still with an instructor.

2 Violence Against Women Happens Every Five Minutes

Out of fear, many women avoid taking part in different various events, because to do so often means being out alone on the road at night. They shy away from lonely places, only go out when accompanied and are often wary about men.

Women, generally, have a particular picture of a potential offender:

- He is a scruffy, brutal looking person.
- He doesn't know his victim and wears dark clothing (e.g., a coat).
- He wears a dark skullcap or a hat that he pulls down to cover his eyes.
- He smells of sweat.
- He speaks vulgarly.
- He is unshaven.
- He seeks women out in lonely places.
- He kills the woman after an attack.

This picture exists in the minds of many women and it is completely wrong. It is, however, a fact that women and girls are at 90% risk within their own social environment. The majority of sexual attacks take place in the family. Women are raped more often than not by their husbands, colleagues, neighbors or friends; girls by their fathers, members of the family, school classmates, neighbors and teachers. The lists are by no means exhaustive. 60% of rapes take place in the woman's apartment. It is a fact that the rapist and the victim more or less know each other already. There is hardly a year that goes by that we don't read about even a church minister who has violated a church server. One would simply not normally associate this kind of person with attacks such as these. What I want to emphasize is that we cannot look into other people's minds and everyone, irrespective of position and upbringing, must be seen as a potential threat.

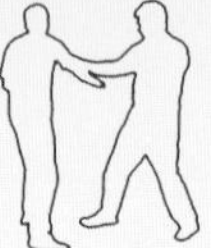

3 Analysis of Attacks on Women

In the following section, I quote several statistics that are prevalent in my home country of Germany. They are included merely as a yardstick and the reader will know or can check on what statistics apply for his/her own area.

3.1 Age structure of the victims

The incidence of attacks against women lies with the ages of 18 – 33 years old. Despite this, in the past there have been incidents of attacks against girls in their infancy and older women of over 80 years old. Again and again, we read of attacks occurring in old people's homes. As one sees, there is no age that is spared from such sexual attacks.

3.2 How have the women been attacked?

The most frequent type of attack was where the woman's skirt had been lifted up or where the culprit had put his hands into the genital area. Second most common was the hug and grabbing/touching the breasts. This was followed by grabbing and knocking the victim down to the ground. In fourth place was the straight fondling of the breasts. About 10% of the women were attacked by a weapon (knife or razor blade, etc.). Then followed attacks on the ground with strangling, strangling of the neck while standing, cuffs around the ears as well as kicks and punches, and also the mouth being held by the hand from behind.

3.3 What was the effect of resistance against attack?

In rape cases, once the victim showed resistance, 70% of the attackers backed off after an attempt. Where resistance was not given, over 90% of rapes were forced through. In 90% of sexual harassment cases, the attacker gave up once resistance was offered. Where resistance was not offered, 60% of the attackers completed their attack (masturbation, fondling, etc.) In the remaining cases, the attackers fled when people disturbed them in the course of the attack. If a woman screams when attacked, there is a danger to the attacker that this will be heard and that someone will come and intervene. Many attackers are put to flight for fear of this. It has also been proved that one should shout "Fire!" rather than "Help!" If a woman shouts out "Fire!" in an apartment block, the neighbors will take note more rapidly – worrying about saving their goods and chattels – and be more willing to help when they find out what is happening.

3.4 What kind of technique is used against sexual molestation or an attempted rape?

About half of all women were able to escape a threatening situation by using verbal aids (talking to the attacker, calling for help and screaming). One in four were able to free themselves from the attacker and make a getaway. 10% used tear gas spray to defend themselves while the remainder punched, kicked or made use of an everyday object such as a long handled hair brush, an umbrella, purse bag, pen or a key.

The interesting fact is, however, that the two most frequently instinctively used methods (screaming and freeing oneself) had an 80% success factor. Nevertheless, the use of self-defense techniques, with and without weapons, was almost always nearly 100% successful.

4 The Offender and the Victim Often Know Each Other

Just about anything you do in the course of normal things could be dangerous, because you never know when a man is planning an attack against you. Remember, about 60% of rape cases take place in the victim's apartment and in about 90% of the cases, the victim and the offender have seen each other once already beforehand.

Example:

- You jog each week at the same time in woodlands.
- You deliver newspapers at night and always use the same route.
- You work in a disco and don't get off work until late at night – you also always park in the same spot.
- .....and so on and so forth.

In all of these situations, a man could be just waiting for an opportune place and time to attack you.

But, there are other situations when it can be dangerous for you, for example:

- Your husband is never at home during the day.

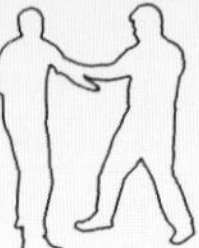

A neighbor or an acquaintance could use this kind of situation and give some reason or other why he is calling on you. Once he has gained access to your apartment it is going to be difficult to stop him.

5 Bringing a Charge Against the Offender

Time and again in my seminars, I have heard of women who have not brought charges after a rape because they were sorry for the man. One course participant told me of a rape case by a workman from the same village. The workman was married and had four children. The woman had had a bad conscience in bringing charges against the man, because the children could lose their father. I don't think men have the same thoughts. Just think about it – this person could well rape the next woman tomorrow. You survived the ordeal – but what about the next woman? Pity really has no place here.

6 Car Breakdown on a Wooded Country Road

Lots of women live in fear of having a breakdown, say, on a wooded road, in the middle of the night. They worry that they could be attacked on the road through the wood. Now, how realistic is this probability that a man has been waiting for years in the wood, waiting for a woman to have a breakdown and wander past him? You can see that this kind of fear is no way justifiable. The real danger lies in the woman's own environment.

It is another thing if, for example, a person is lying in the road and she is forced to halt. In this case, she should lock the doors from inside and then, if alone on the road, really think whether she should get out of the vehicle or not. In Germany (other countries may have different rules), you are bound by law to render assistance, but not necessarily put yourself in danger by doing so. Therefore, the best thing is to stay in the vehicle at a reasonable distance away and make a call to the police on your cell phone. If you don't have one available, then drive on to the next place and initiate an emergency call.

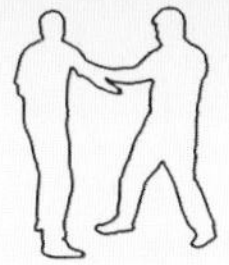

7 How Should a Woman React in a Threatening Situation?

As you will have read in the preceding sections, the types of attack that you can be subject to are so various that there is no panacea for a general way of reacting in a threatening situation. There are, however, a few things that can be crystallized from the subject matter covered so far.

- If a woman defends herself in an attack (including verbal resistance) then there is high probability (90%) that the offender will put to flight. The chance of success is increased considerably if the woman uses some appropriate defensive techniques.

- A confident attitude (shoulders squared, eyebrows raised and eyes wide open, etc.) will almost always put off an attacker from doing his deed.

- If the woman doesn't defend herself (verbally or physically) then an attacker will almost certainly carry on with his attack. This means not only in the case of a rape but also with cases of sexual harassment in the workplace. If a woman doesn't react and complain when a colleague continually is touching her bottom, then he will not stop doing it and rather start to do other things. The sooner a woman can set her 'limits', the more successful she'll be.

- When a woman defends herself, the level of brutality is seldom increased.

Analyzing all the texts above leads one to conclude that, as a general rule, resistance always brings a positive result and passiveness a negative result.

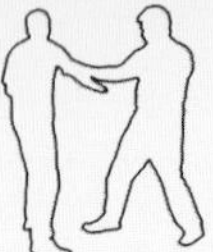

8 Sexual Harassment on the Bus, Train or also in the Office

If a man lays his hand on your thigh, you can grab hold of it and lift it right up, calling out loud, "Whose hand is this on my thigh?" This way you will have made a fool of the harasser and he will probably leave off. Otherwise, in the following sections, you will learn some techniques that you can use to react.

If a man fumbles you in a crowd or crush (in the train, the bus or the streetcar), you can rub the outside of your shoe down his shins and rip his skin. Another possibility is to stand forcibly on his foot with the pointed heel of your shoe.

9 Provocative Clothing

A self-assured woman will not be told what she should wear and when. However, there are occasions when perhaps it would be more suitable to wear flat shoes, because you can run better with them. On a long, unlit street to the dance club, it would be better perhaps to put the dancing shoes in a carrier and cover up the mini skirt under a coat.

By wearing certain items (mini skirt, push-up bra, high heels, etc.) you automatically attract a man's attention. This is perhaps exactly what you want to do otherwise you wouldn't wear them. It's true that the enticement of a woman's clothing alone should be no reason for him to rape the woman. There is, of course, no danger from most men; however, there are one or two who have no self-control and cannot resist the enticement.

In my courses, I always ask the women whether they lock their cars, the house and the windows at night. Some ask, "Why?" It is against the law to take things from a stranger's house and it's also not allowed to steal a car radio. So, why do you lock the house up? - Quite simply to prevent a thief from clearing out the house or the car.

Just park a car in a remote place and I bet that within a week it will have no tires (probably within two days) and that by the end of the week the vehicle will have been completely gutted.

10 Exhibitionists

Winter has past and it is getting warmer and warmer. As the weather changes, press reports of men showing themselves increase. As a rule, only the men themselves get a kick out of showing their naked parts and they are actually afraid of women. In such cases, follow-up attacks are seldom. You should ignore the man, carry on your way and immediately notify the police. After all, it is possible that the man will attempt to rape the next passing woman. Don't stand there and laugh at him or tell him how ridiculous he looks. This could make him aggressive and such a situation should be avoided at all costs.

C THE PRACTICAL SECTION

1 Training Tips

- First of all, only the steps of the exercise should be gone through. In this, the partner does not offer any resistance. Only when the steps of the exercise have been mastered do you then flesh out the partner's resistance (70%) to see how the technique functions.
- When the technique has been learned, it should be 'tested' on someone who is not so technically proficient (an inexperienced beginner) and who is lighter. Doing this allows you to use what you have learned without being faced with effective counter techniques. If the partner is more experienced and perhaps heavier then there is a danger that the new techniques will not be effective (because they cannot be used properly) and you don't carry on exercising with them.
- If, in training, a technique is not effective because you don't understand how it works, it is best to take a time-out (e.g., have a drink or go to the toilet). In such a case it could be that there is a brain block in play (left side/right side brain block). Each side of the brain has its separate function. In many people, the left half of the brain controls the logic, ability to analyze, language, numeracy, thought linearity and other abilities. The right half of the brain controls rhythm, perceptibility, dimension and fantasy amongst other abilities. In order to be able to work through a sequence of movements, both halves of the brain have to work together. In stress situations, or when under strain (which also causes stress), this doesn't function. Movement can relieve this block. This 'method' can also be used in situations of everyday problems. Also the double-stick training in Kali (Arnis and Eskrima) contributes to the improvement of these abilities. When complex exercises that require use of both halves of the brain are repeated often, additional connections can be formed between both the halves (so-called "synapses"). This then makes it possible for us to perform the exercise sequences more quickly. Studies of the brain have shown, for example, that by performing rhythmic exercise sequences (right half of the brain) the speech process can also be improved (left half of the brain). Thus, the stimulation of the functions of one half of the brain can also benefit the other.

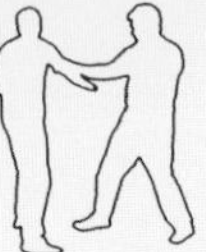

On the other hand, these pauses offer a good opportunity to consider what has been learned and to prepare for what lies ahead. However, these pauses should not be longer than 10 minutes. In order to optimize learning, the first short pause should already take place after approximately 60 minutes of training.

- Shortly after completion of training, the material learned can still be recalled. A day later it is already almost impossible to remember all the details. The ability to remember also has to do with how much interest one has shown in following all of the training. Things that are very interesting to someone remain in their memory more readily than the things that are not. For this reason, it is advisable that directly after the training the material that has been learned be reviewed (consolidated) and written down. It should be repeated the next day again and, if necessary, supplemented.
- Making notes helps the training to be processed mentally. One way is for the learner to read the description of the technique aloud and visualize the situation, similar to the way used in "shadowboxing." Another method is for the learner to imagine the whole situation. He sees himself in his thoughts – like in a film – in action – and lives through the previous day's combinations. One can also record the notes on a cassette or CD and listen to them (for example, while commuting or at home). While one listens to the text, one should envisage the situation as colorfully as possible. So that one can note something especially well, it is advantageous to utilize as many senses as possible simultaneously. With this I mean not only the visual or acoustical senses, but above all also the sense of feeling. Things stay considerably better in my memory if I imagine the effect of a lever or a stranglehold intensely, rather than if I only hear the text. Exaggeration is also a method to use to better remember what has been learned. In this way, the time required adapting to a combination or this mental training can shorten a technique sequence.
- Positive thinking is necessary in order to be successful. If the trainee becomes negatively influenced before the lesson ("the other person is so big, so awfully strong, and also looks so dangerous..."), he won't often be successful because he has already given up in advance. If a human positively motivates himself before a task (and that involves not only for sport), it will be considerably easier for him to reach his goal.
- In order to be successful (and not only for sport), the setting of goals is also an important point. It makes sense to formulate short-, middle- and long-term goals. These should however be realistic, i.e., something that is

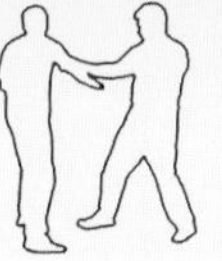

attainable. One can write the goals on a note and stick it (for example) to the bathroom mirror so that one is constantly reminded. A goal could be: "I will win the next championship."

- Autogenic training helps in the fulfillment of these set goals. Here, the trainee always replaces a negative goal with a positive statement (a motto, for example) that he can accept in his subconscious. These should always be positively worded. Wrong would be: "I have no fear." Better: "I can do it!" Or: "I am brave." The reason lies in the fact that these formulations are automatically recalled in certain situations. For this area, as for that of mental training, there is an abundance of literature.

2 Step Work

In many of the Philippine Martial Arts Systems you will find the following step work:

- Forward on guard stance – male
- Female on guard stance
- Cat stance

2.1 Forward on guard stance - male

In the forward on guard stance the point of triangular axis of the feet is pointing at the attacker. Your weight is either on the forward or rear foot. To change over from a right stance to a left stance, the rear foot is brought forward and the forward foot is placed to the rear.

1

2

3

2.2 Female on guard stance

In the female on guard stance the point of triangular axis of the feet is pointing at the defender. Your weight is either on the forward or rearward foot. To change over from a right stance to a left stance, the forward foot is brought to the rear and the rear foot is placed forward.

1

2

3

2.3 Cat stance

In the cat stance, 80% of your weight is placed on the rear leg. The defender is standing at an angle of about 90° to the attacker.

1

2

3

3 'Neutral' Defensive Positions

When practicing martial arts and you are standing in front of the attacker in a fighting stance, then in my opinion you have already lost a major part of the advantage over him. Your defense will be more successful and easier if you can make him feel secure and not expecting an attack. Therefore, in the following sections I would like to introduce you to a few stances that don't exactly give away the fact that you follow martial arts or that you know anything about self-defense.

3.1 Speaking with your hands

Bring your hands up in front of your body and "speak" with them so that the attacker cannot get to your body without having to push your hands to one side beforehand.

3.2 The Thinker

Bring one hand up to your chin and stretch out the forefinger. This will give the impression that you are listening to the attacker.

3.3 The Door Guard

Cross you arms over in front of your chest. When doing this don't intertwine them but lay one arm on top of the other, otherwise you could have problems moving one of your arms outwards in time to do a blocking technique.

3.4 The Minister

Place your palms together as if you are praying and speak to the attacker saying that he should not go on to attack you. From this position, you are well placed to be able to carry out simultaneous blocking and hindering techniques such as a finger jab to the eyes.

3.5 The TV Presenter

When a TV presenter begins to host a show, he often emphasizes his statements by employing a positive body language. He lifts his hands with the palms upwards. The arms are angled out at about 45°. Similarly, you are able to carry out blocking and shock techniques from this stance.

It is important that in all these stances that the arms are kept in the upper half of the body, thus giving you a chance to be able to defend against a strike with a block. If your arms are grasped together behind your body or are hanging down your sides, you will not come through a surprise attack e.g., a knife attack at your throat.

4 Blocking Techniques

As a general rule, blocking techniques should be carried out so that the side of the hand with the little finger is the one that comes up against the weapon-holding hand (palm down block). This increases the probability of lesser injuries being suffered when the attacker pulls the weapon back.

A worst case is where the defender blocks the weapon holding arm with the inside of his hand. Should the attacker pull his knife back, then there is a chance that the artery could be cut open. A better, but not exactly optimum way of blocking is with the back of the hand. However, in such a case, the wound will be right across the back of the hand or the lower arm. Blocking techniques are used generally when the defender (D) is very close to the attacker where he (D) cannot carry out a sweeping movement with his hand or arm.

To carry out a block technique in the event of an attack, the defender should always use the arm nearest to the attacker's weapon-holding arm in order to make best use of his natural reflexes. Taking hold of the weapon-bearing arm diagonally demands a great deal from your coordinative ability and should be practiced only as a second phase. Because your reaction in many instances is carried as a reflex, you should always prepare for the worst and practice the blocking techniques, even for use in cases where there is no weapon.

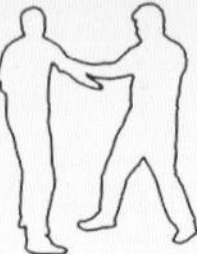

5 Sweeping Techniques

Sweeping techniques can be done both on the forehand and the backhand. For your own safety, with sweeping techniques, it is also recommended that you use the back of the hand to sweep away knife attacks. As before, the injuries you may suffer will be less if the attacker pulls his knife back. Sweeping techniques can also be done diagonally, that is, against a right-handed attack the defender counters with his right hand. As I have already mentioned, this calls for a great deal of coordinative ability on the part of the defender, because as the arm crosses over the center line of the body, its control is transferred from one side of the brain to the other. Not everyone is capable of this coordination and can react quickly enough - you have to work at achieving the ability to carry out this movement. The attack, generally, happens so rapidly that we are only able to react reflexively. In conclusion and as always, and presuming a serious attack (knife wound/stab), carry on practicing the sweeping movements as described above, also for cases where no weapons are involved.

6 Using Blocking and Sweeping Techniques

The use of blocking and sweeping techniques depends on the distance (reach) between the attacker and the defender. Here's an explanation of this:

As a basic rule, the beginner should start on this using the following principles:

Basic principles for the use of blocking and sweeping techniques:

- Use the arm closest to the opponent's attacking arm in order to make use of one's natural reflexes.
- The flat of the hand, in a blocking or sweeping technique, is pointing (as far as is possible) towards the ground in order to minimize the danger of suffering a possible wound (in a knife attack).
- The defender should always try to get around to the outside of the attacker, because in this position it is less dangerous than when the defender stands directly in front the attacker.

7 Ranges/Reach

As is general in self-defense, when weapons are involved one speaks of various distances (reaches).

7.1 Long reach

With the hand stretched out, the attacker cannot touch the defender.

7.2 Middle reach

With the hand stretched out, the attacker can touch the defender's nose.

7.3 Close reach

With the hand stretched out, the attacker can touch the defender's ear.

7.4 Throwing and groundwork reaches

With the hand stretched out, the attacker can touch the defender's neck.

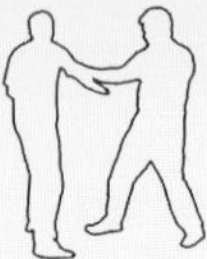

8 The Concepts of Using Different Reaches

- Anticipating
- Spoiling tactics
- Dodging
- Gunting
- Sweeping actions
- Sweeping actions and Gunting
- Blocking
- Blocking and punching or kicking techniques
- Gripping
- Gripping and punching or kicking techniques

8.1 Anticipating

The most effective way of surviving an attack without injury is to anticipate what the attacker will do (interception). This concept can be used at any of the reaches. If the attacker has convinced you that he is about to attack or has a weapon in his hand, then the defender is justified in using defensive force because an attack is imminent and this would be a criminal act. The defender should immediately employ an effective technique against one of the attacker's vital points (eyes, nose, larynx or genitals). Once you can see the pain in the attacker's eyes, the defender should bridge the distance (for example, by raining blows down onto the attacker) to his face and continue with his defense. Further on in this book, several examples are included.

8.2 Spoiling tactics

The second way is to attack the opponent's extremities (destruction).

Examples:

1. Attacker (A) delivers a punch at defender's (D) head.
2. D uses an 'Oh-shit block' by covering his face with his right lower arm and directs his right elbow towards the attacking fist.

1. A delivers a low kick at the outside of D's left thigh.
2. D angles his left leg sharply up and directs his knee against A's right shin.

1. A delivers a sideways kick at D's stomach with his right foot.
2. D carries out an upwards strike with his elbow at A's right thigh/ankle.

In the actions seen, you can also close the reach by raining punches down on the attacker after you note that you have caused him some pain. You then have an opportunity of following this up with further techniques (such as those shown later on in this book).

8.3 Dodging

Dodging is best done at a long reach distance.

8.4 Gunting

At this distance, the attacker and the defender are standing in a long or middle reach. Dependent on whether the defender is carrying a knife, he either slits or strikes the attacking arm (Gunting = term for 'scissors'). In the Gunting reach (striking vital points) you cause the attacker some pain, and then as soon as you see that this has happened, this creates the possibility for you to go to work on him. The Gunting technique is not quite as forceful as the 'spoiling tactics' above. If you strike the target you will distract his concentration but you won't bring him into submission.

8.5 Sweeping actions

Sweeping techniques are used mainly in the middle reach distance. The defender best uses the backhand or at least the side of the hand with the little finger.

8.6 Sweeping actions and Gunting

The defender uses a sweeping technique and a strike technique together. This kind of combination is mainly used in the middle reach distance.

8.7 Blocking

For example, A is holding a knife and uses it to strike in Attack Angle #1 (inwards to the head). D is at close reach distance. As a result it is difficult to push the weapon-carrying arm sideways with a sweeping motion. D blocks the attack using his arm nearest to the attacker.

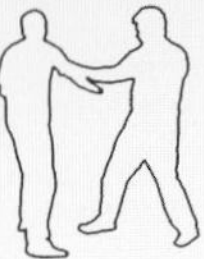

8.8 Blocking and punching or kicking techniques

For example, A is holding a knife and uses it to strike in Attack Angle #1 (inwards to the head) or delivers a swinging punch. D is at close reach distance. As a result it is difficult to push the weapon-carrying arm sideways with a sweeping motion. D blocks the attack using his arm nearest to the attacker and at the same time, using his free hand, he carries out a strike to either shock the attacker with it, or he kicks out with his leg.

8.9 Gripping

For example, A is holding a knife and uses it to strike in Attack Angle #1 (inwards to the head) or delivers a swinging punch. D is at close reach distance. As a result it is difficult to push the weapon-carrying arm sideways with a sweeping motion. D grabs hold of the attacking arm with both hands and brings them under control.

8.10 Gripping and kicking or punching techniques

For example, A is holding a knife and uses it to strike in Attack Angle #1 (inwards to the head) or delivers a swinging punch at D's head. D is at close reach distance. As a result it is difficult to push the weapon-carrying arm sideways with a sweeping motion. D grabs hold of the attacking arm with both hands and brings them under control. Then, first of all he delivers a kicking technique and follows this up with a punching technique or a head butt.

9 Falling Techniques

9.1 Forward roll

If you are pushed from behind down to the ground, the best thing to do is a forward roll.

1. D is standing in the start position...
2. ...and places his right leg forward a pace, bringing his right hand down between his own legs.
3. He then supports himself on the ground with his left hand and places the little finger of the right hand on to the ground. The fingers of the right hand point towards the gap between his legs.
4. D rolls over onto his right shoulder (NB: not over his head!)...
5. ...and comes up with his left leg kneeling on the ground and places his right foot forward down onto the ground. It would be better if you can come up directly onto your feet as this will reduce any danger of suffering injury to your legs. This requires regular practice though and that is why I have illustrated the simpler method here.
6. D stands up and turns around in the direction of the attacker.

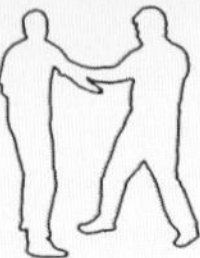

9.2 Backward roll

If someone in front of you pushes you down to the ground, the best thing to do is a backward roll.

1. D is standing in the start position...
2. ...and kneels down on to his right knee...
3. ...falls backwards and rolls over his left shoulder...
4. ...ending up kneeling on his left knee and supporting himself with both arms.
5. He then stands up.

As in the forward roll it is less dangerous if you don't kneel but come up straight away onto your feet. This way of doing it is, however, more difficult and requires regular practice and that is why I have illustrated the simpler method here.

9.3 Falling sideways

Falling sideways techniques are required, for example, when the defender has been thrown over the attacker's hips.

Preparatory exercise:

For the beginner, it is best to practice this from the crouch position and it should be practiced to the left and to the right.

1. D crouches down...

2. ...and stretches his left leg out to the right side...

3. ...and lets himself fall down to the left. As he does this he keeps his left leg stretched out. D slaps the ground with his left hand stretched out as it reaches the ground so that he absorbs the energy from the fall.

4. D angles his left leg back to protect his genitals from a possible kick and brings his arms up to give cover to his body.

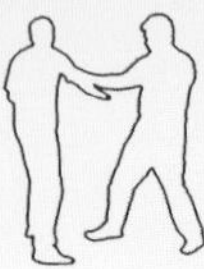

From a standing position:

1. D stretches his left leg out to the right side...
2. ...and lets himself fall down to the left. As he does this he keeps his left leg stretched out. D slaps the ground with his left hand stretched out as it reaches the ground so that he absorbs the energy from the fall.
3. D angles his left leg back to protect his genitals from a possible kick and brings his arms up to cover his body.

Avoid the following mistakes:

- Trying to save yourself using the stretched out arm.

1. D stretches his left leg out to the right side.
2. D tries to save the fall by stretching out his left arm. There is a grave danger that he could injure his shoulder or his wrist by doing this.

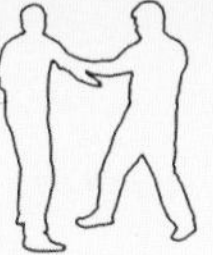

- Trying to save yourself using a bent arm.

1. D stretches his left leg out to the right side.
2. D tries to save the fall by landing on his left bent arm. There is a grave danger that he could injure his shoulder, elbow or his wrist by doing this.

- Defending yourself as you stand up

1. D is lying on the left side of his body. Here, we must imagine that A is standing in front of D.
2. D kicks out sideways with his right foot at A's shin/knee.

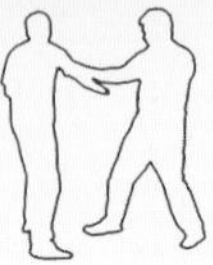

3. He then props his right leg up, positioning both hands rearwards on the ground to the left...

4. ...and pulls himself up into a firm position.

5. D places his right leg down forwards...

6. ...and could deliver (if necessary) a further sideways kick at A's legs from this firm position.

7. He then stands up.

9.4 Falling forwards

Preparatory exercise

From a standing position

9.5 Falling backwards

Preparatory exercise

From a standing position

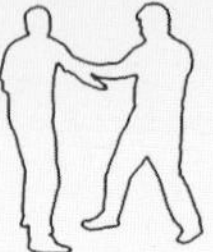

10 Unarmed Self-Defense

In this section we cover the following:

- Close contact fighting
- Attacks with no contact
- Particular situations (in the bar, in a vehicle)
- Attacks on the ground
- Knife attacks
- Stick attacks
- Use of everyday objects to defend yourself with

10.1 Close contact fighting

This means that the attacker has got hold of you. This is the normal case for women. With men, the attacks take place primarily without contact (i.e., they start with punches and kicks).

Close contact fights include (selected list):

Grabbing hold of the wrist
- Opposite
- Diagonally
- Both wrists
- From the front
- From behind
- Both hands
- One wrist
- From the front
- From behind

Grabbing the hair
- From the front
- From the side
- From behind

Grabbing hold of the lapels/breasts
- From the front
- From behind

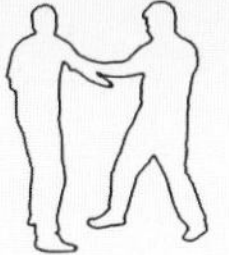

Embrace/Clinch/Bear hug

- From the front
- Over the arms
- Under the arms
- From behind
- Over the arms
- Under the arms

The unwelcome embrace/ Linking the arm

- Being grabbed around the waist

Collar being grabbed from behind

- Single handed
- Double handed

Stranglehold attacks

- From the front
- From behind
- By use of the lower arm
- When on the ground
- Attacker is on his back
- Attacker is lying between your legs
- Attacker is lying on his side
- Attacker is behind your head
- Attacker is sitting on your stomach

10.1.1 Defensive combinations against close contact attacks

In the combinations I list here, I assume that these are split second situations in a scuffle and that the danger for the person being attacked is very high. I also assume that the defender is physically weaker than the attacker by far. The sequences of the techniques are very effective, but quite dangerous for the attacker, who can often be injured quite severely by their use. Always remember that your defense must be relative to the attack. Try to resolve a conflict always by choosing the verbal route first.

The combinations have to be effective. But you should not have to hesitate about which one you will use. Therefore, I have chosen techniques here where the physique of the attacker doesn't play any particular role, because the parts of the eyes, larynx, nose, ears and genitals in the human are not dependent on his muscle mass, and all are equally sensitive.

Being grabbed hold of by the opponent's opposite hand

1. A grabs hold of D's right hand with his left hand.

2. Using the left hand, D delivers a finger jab at A's neck and brings her right hand further outwards (Tan Sao)...

3. ...and strikes D's thumb with the left hand...

4. ...then uses the right hand to slap the left hand side of A's face with the open hand.

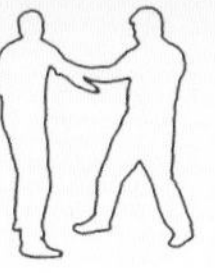

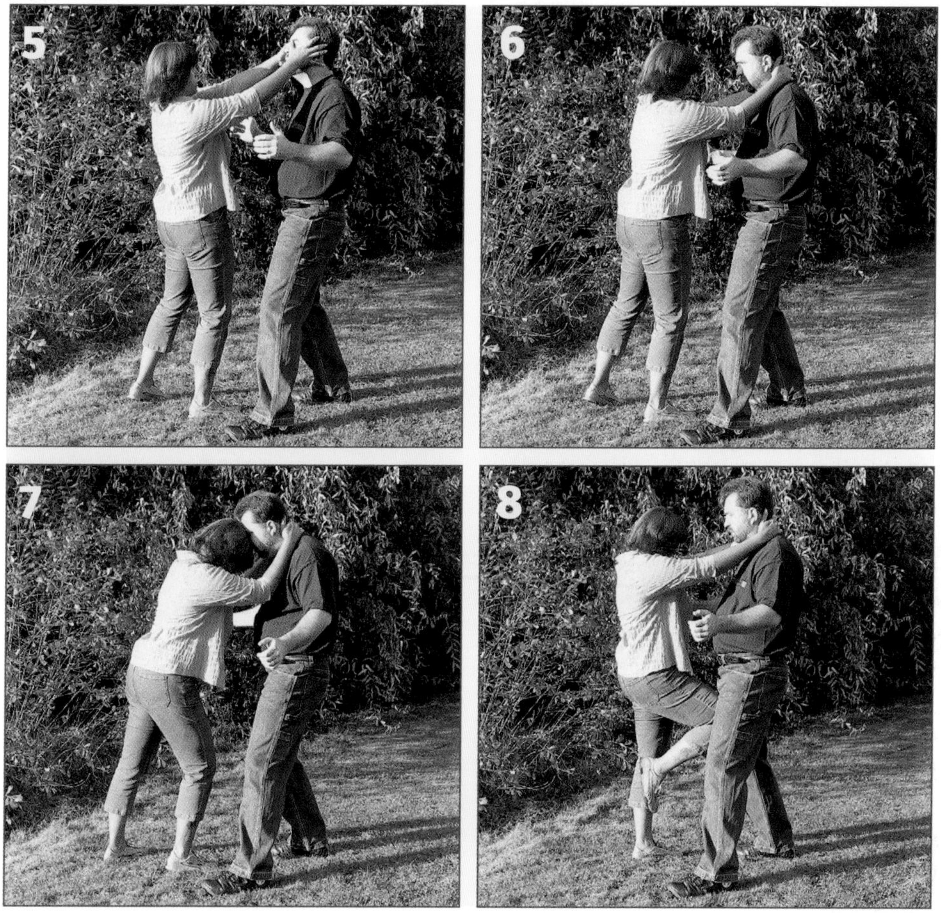

5. She now brings both her thumbs over A's eyes...

6. ...and grabs hold of A's head in both hands...

7. doing a head butt at A's head...

8. ...followed by a knee-up kick at the genitals...

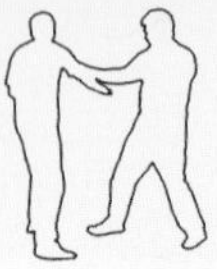

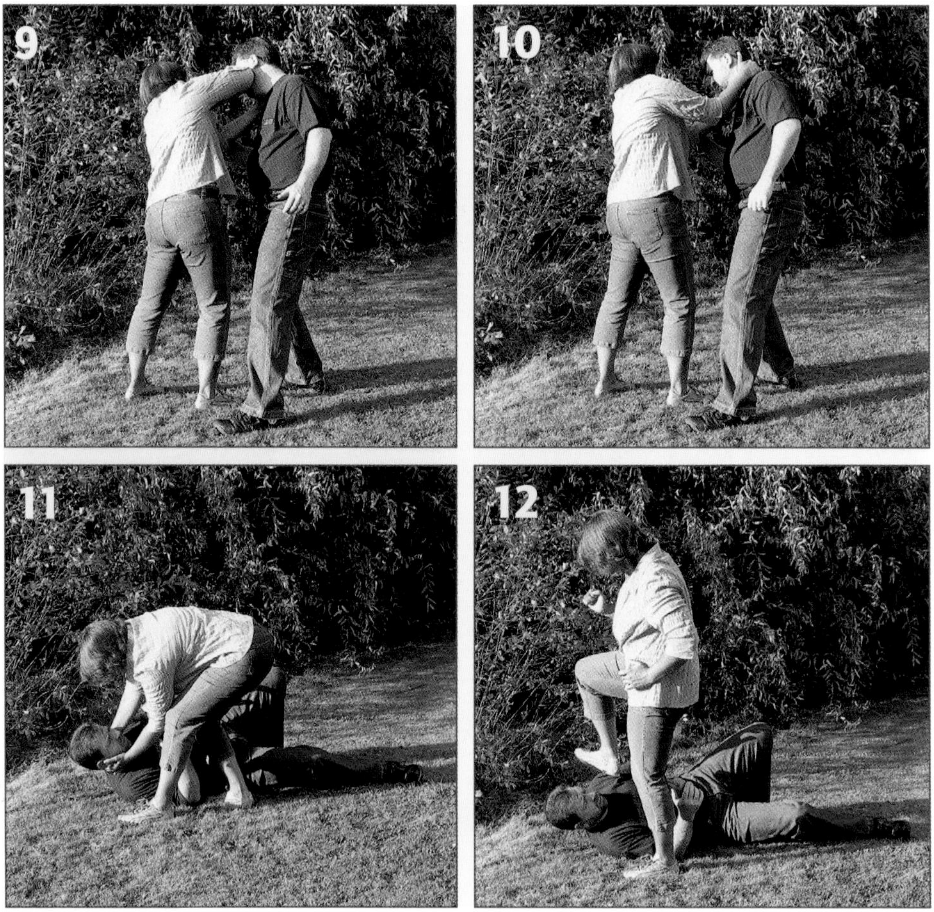

9. ...and a strike with the right elbow at A's head.

10. D grabs hold of A's neck in both hands...

11. ...and pushes A down onto the ground...

12. ...ending the combination by stamping down on A's head with the foot.

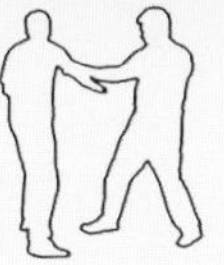

Being grabbed hold of by the opponent's diagonal hand

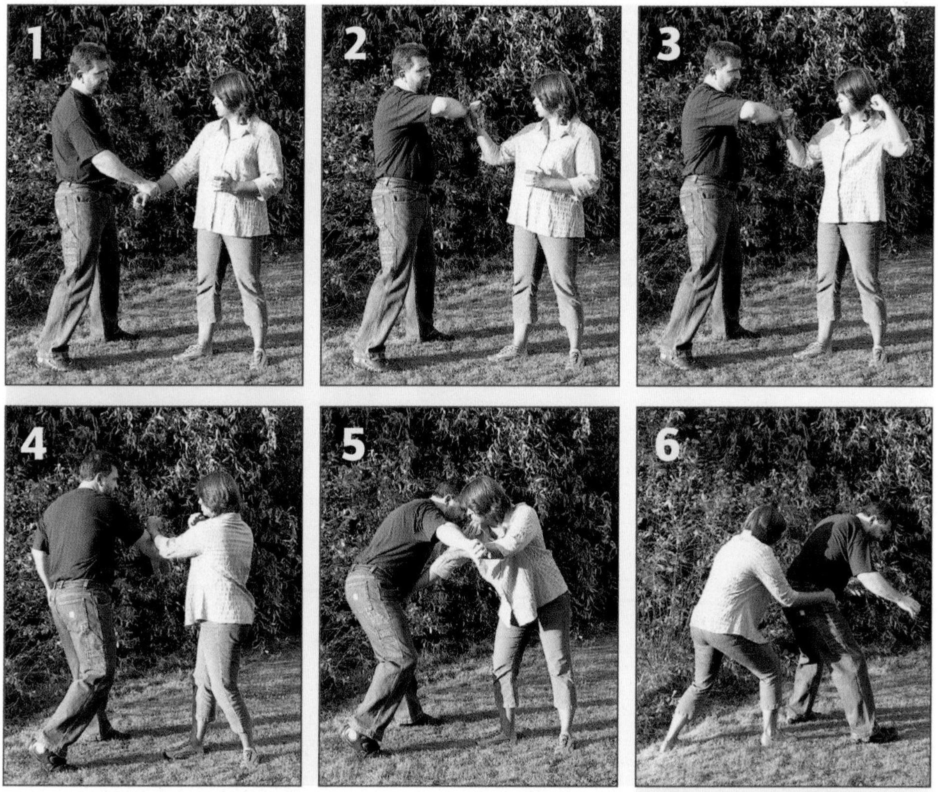

1. A grabs hold of D's right hand with his right hand.
2. D brings her right hand upwards clockwise...
3. ...and delivers a left-handed punch inwards at A's right hand...
4. ...carries out a right-handed punch at A's genitals causing A to bend over forward.
5. D gets around behind A and places the middle finger of both hands in A's crutches...
6. ...and pulls A at an angle of 45° down to the ground...
7. ...ending the combination by stamping down on A's head with the foot.

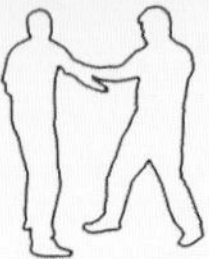

Being grabbed from the front and being held by both of the opponent's hands

1. A grabs hold of D's hands using both of his hands.
2. D carries out a head butt at A's head...
3. ...and executes a double-handed freeing movement...
4. ...ending by grabbing hold of both of A's wrists.
5. She then delivers a knee-up kick at A's genitals.
6. D delivers a right-legged kick at A's forward knee...
7. ...making A fall down.
8. D finishes the combination by stamping down with her foot on A's ankle.

Being grabbed and held by both of the opponent's hands from behind

1. Standing behind D, A grabs hold of both her wrists with his hands.
2. D pulls her right leg up to gain momentum...
3. ...and delivers a right-legged kick backwards at A's knee.
4. D then presses her left lower arm against A's left thumb and pulls it forward in a freeing movement.
5. D turns around clockwise to face A...

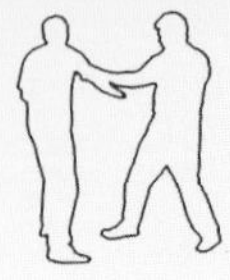

6. ...and brings her right hand upwards clockwise...
7. ...and punches A's right hand away to the inside...
8. ...followed up by a right-handed punch at A's genitals with the right hand, causing A to bend over forwards.
9. D gets around behind A and places the middle finger of both hands in A's crutches...
10. ...and pulls A at an angle of 45° down to the ground, ending the combination by stamping down on A's head with the foot.

Being grabbed from the front and the wrist held by both of the opponent's hands

1 2 3

4 5 6

1. A grabs hold of D's wrist in both of his hands.
2. Using the left lower arm, D strikes A's arm downwards...
3. ...and simultaneously does a freeing movement with the right hand in the direction of A's thumb.
4. D does a right-handed punch at A's head...
5. ...brings her thumbs over A's eyes...
6. ...and takes hold of A's head in both hands...

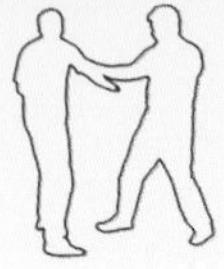

7. ...and delivers a head butt at A's head.

8. As she lifts the head back up, she does a knee-up kick at A's genitals...

9. ...and then a right elbow strike at A's head...

10. ...grabs hold of A's neck in both hands and pressing on his neck brings him to the ground...

11. ...ending the combination by stamping down on A's head with her right foot.

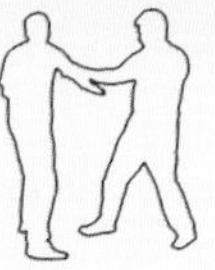

Being grabbed from behind and the wrist held by both of the opponent's hands

1 2 3 4 5 6

1. From behind, A grabs hold of D's wrist in both of his hands.
2. D turns around clockwise to face A...
3. ...and using the left lower arm, D strikes A's arm downwards...
4. ...and simultaneously does a freeing movement with the left hand in the direction of A's thumb.
5. D does a further left-handed punch at A's head...
6. ...brings her thumbs over A's eyes...

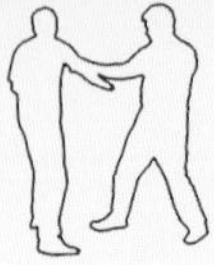

7. ...and takes hold of A's head in both hands...

8. ...and delivers a head butt at A's head.

9. As she lifts the head back up, she does a knee-up kick at A's genitals...

10. ...and then a right elbow strike at A's head...

11. ...grabs hold of A's neck in both hands and pressing on his neck brings him to the ground...

12. ...ending the combination by stamping down on A's head with her right foot.

Being grabbed by the hair from the front by the opponent

1. Facing her, A grabs hold of D's hair with his right hand.
2. D brings a right-handed punch down on A's nose...
3. ...and then another punch at A's genitals and...
4. ...bringing her left hand back to gain momentum...
5. ...punches A's right hand away inside with her left hand...
6. ...simultaneously delivering a right elbow strike at A's liver.
7. D gets around behind A and grabs his head and eyes in both hands...
8. ...and using a twisting throw jerking the body, brings him backwards down onto the ground. D ends the combination by stamping down on A's head with her foot.

Being grabbed by the hair from the side by the opponent

1. A is standing at right angles to D and grabs hold of her hair from the side.
2. D delivers a finger jab with the right hand to A's eyes...
3. ...turns around clockwise to face A and stands next to him at a right angle.
4. With her right hand, D grabs hold of A's testicles and pushes her left hand into A's face.
5. By pulling at his testicles with the right hand and pushing his face with the left hand, she causes A to fall over backwards.
6. A stamping kick down on A's upper body with her right foot ends the combination.

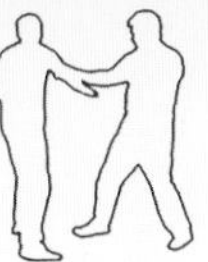

Being grabbed by the hair from behind by the opponent

1. Standing behind D, A grabs hold of her hair.
2. At an angle of 45°, D takes a step backwards with her left leg past A's right leg...
3. ...turns around clockwise and positions herself next to him at right angles. She places her left arm and hand around behind A's waist.
4. D delivers a punch with the fist (hammer strike) at the genitals...
5. ...grabs hold of the testicles in the right hand and pushes her left hand into A's face.
6. By pulling at his testicles with the right hand and pushing his face with the left hand, she causes A to fall over backwards.
7. A stamping kick down on A's upper body with her right foot ends the combination.

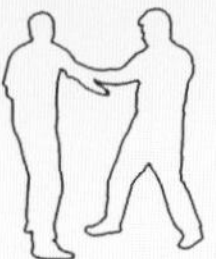

Being grabbed hold of by the collar/scarf from behind by the opponent

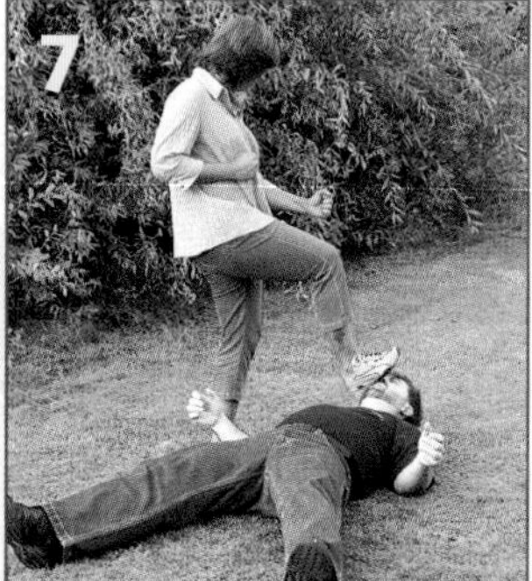

1. From behind, A grabs D's collar with the right hand.
2. D jumps around quickly counter-clockwise to face A so that his fingers could be twisted and be broken in the collar.
3. D brings her right arm back to gain momentum...
4. ...and delivers a right-handed punch (hammer strike) at the genitals...
5. ...grabs hold of the testicles in the right hand and pushes her left hand into A's face.
6. By pulling at his testicles with the right hand and pushing his face with the left hand, she causes A to fall over backwards.
7. A stamping kick down on A's upper body with her right foot ends the combination.

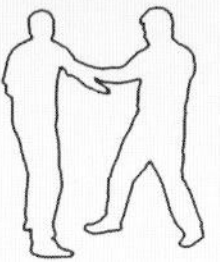

Being grabbed hold of by the lapels/breasts by the opponent facing you

1. With both hands, A grabs hold of D's lapel. D pulls both arms back to gain momentum...
2. ...and presses her hands hard against A's head to create pressure in the ears.
3. D brings both thumbs over A's eyes...
4. ...and grabs hold of the back of his head...
5. ...and does a head butt.

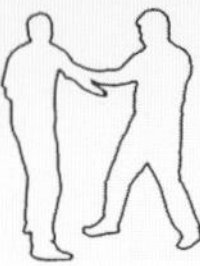

6. As she lifts the head back up, she does a knee-up kick at A's genitals...

7. ...and then a right elbow strike at A's head...

8. ...grabs hold of A's neck in both hands...

9. ... and pressing on his neck brings him to the ground ending the combination by stamping down on A's head with her right foot.

Being grabbed hold of by the lapels/breasts under the arms from behind

1. A reaches around under D's arms from behind and grabs hold of D's lapels in both hands.

2. D executes a strike with the right elbow backwards at A's head...

3. ...and with her left hand, D grabs hold of the little finger of A's left hand...

4. ...and pushes it back in the direction of A's left lower arm (finger dislocating) thus freeing herself from the grip.

5. D delivers a right-fisted punch at A's head...

6. ...followed by a further punch at the head with the left fist...

7. ...and then finally another right-fisted punch at A's head (i.e., chain of blows).

8. D brings both thumbs over A's eyes...

9. ...grabs the back of A's head in both hands...

10. ...and does a head butt at A's head.

11. With an upwards jerk of the leg, D knees A in the genitals...

12. ...carries out a right elbow strike at A's head...

13. ...grabs hold of the back of A's neck and brings him down to the ground by pressing his neck downwards.

14. D ends the combination by delivering a stamping kick at A's head.

Bear hug frontally pinning down the arms

1. A takes D into a bear hug over the arms from the front.
2. D brings her head back to gain momentum...
3. ...and does a head butt at A's head.
4. Placing both hands on A's hips...

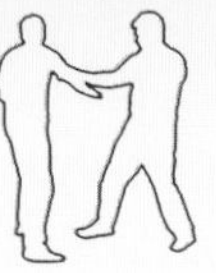

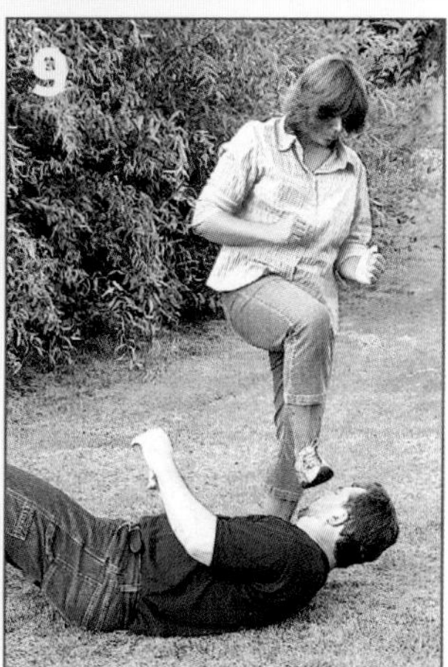

5. ...hunches down and away at an angle of 45°...

6. ...and with her right leg knees up into A's genitals.

7. D carries out a right elbow strike at A's head...

8. ...grabs hold of the back of A's neck with both hands and twists his head in the direction of the ground...

9. ...ending the combination by stamping down on A's head with the right foot.

Bear hug frontally reaching under the arms

1. A takes D into a bear hug under the arms from the front.
2. D brings both her arms back to gain momentum...
3. ...and does a pressure clamp on the ears of A's head.
4. D grabs hold of the A's ears with her fingers...
5. ...pulls them forward and brings her head back to gain momentum...

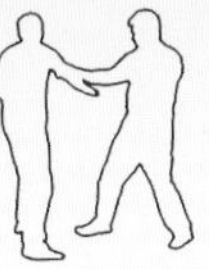

6. ...and delivers a head butt at A.

7. D does a knee-up into A's genitals...

8. ...places her left hand on the chin and her right hand around the back of the neck...

9. ...and twists A's head around in an anticlockwise direction...

10. ...and using this lever brings him down to the ground. D stamps down on A's head to end the combination.

Bear hug from behind pinning down the arms

1. A takes D into a bear hug over the arms from behind.

2. D brings her head forward to gain momentum...

3. ...and does a head butt backwards at A's head...

4. ...and then places the right foot outwards to the right...

5. ...and swings her bottom forwards and...

6. ...then pushes it sharply backwards at A's genitals, freeing herself from A's grip as she does this.

7. D grabs hold of A's forward leg in both hands...

8. ...and sits down on A's thigh pulling his leg upwards with both hands as she does this.

9. Kicking backwards at A's genitals, D ends the combination.

Bear hug from behind reaching under the arms

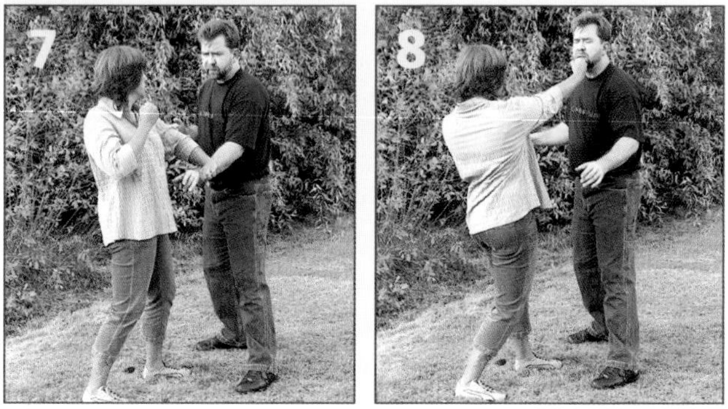

1. A takes D into a bear hug under the arms from behind.
2. D brings her head forward to gain momentum...
3. ...and does a head butt backwards at A's head...
4. ...and then lifts her left foot upwards...
5. ...followed by stamping it down on A's left foot.
6. With her left hand, D grabs hold of A's little finger of his left hand
7. ...and pushes this in the direction of A's left lower arm (finger dislocating) and frees herself by twisting away anticlockwise outwards to the left.
8. D delivers a right-fisted punch at A's head...

9. ...then a left-fisted punch at A's head...
10. ...followed up with another right-fisted punch at his head (chain blows).
11. D places both thumbs over A's eyes...
12. ...grabs A's head in both hands...
13. ...and does a head butt at A's head...
14. ...and a knee-up right-legged kick in the genitals.
15. This followed by a strike with the right elbow at A's head...
16. ...D then twists A's head...
17. ...and brings A down to the ground. D stamps his foot down on A's head to end the combination.

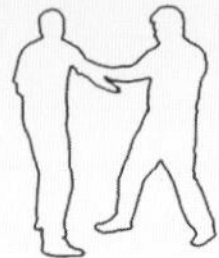

The unwelcome embrace

1. A is standing on D's left-hand side and has placed his right arm around D's shoulders.
2. D brings up her left arm to gain momentum...
3. ...and delivers a hammering left-fisted punch into A's genitals.
4. D raises the thumb of the left hand and...
5. ...brings the arm up sharply jabbing the left thumb into A's right eye.
6. D brings her left arm around the back of A's neck...

7. ...and with the right hand she takes A by the throat (larynx)...

8. ...and using this stranglehold brings A down to the ground; this is very dangerous for A because twisting the larynx can cause death.

9. A downward kick ends the combination.

At this juncture, I would like to point out that the suggested combinations are taken from a given situation. For all the combinations, no account will be taken of what the attacker has to say. If, for example, a man takes hold of a woman and it becomes clear that the woman is about to be raped, then one is faced with an ongoing criminal situation. Since the woman will be physically weaker than the man, she will not be successful in using only simple defense techniques. Therefore the suggested combinations can prove to be a way for the woman to be able to defend herself. One could also have the situation where a man is surrounded by several others, and one of them grabs hold of the defender's arm and it becomes clear, from what the man is saying, that he is about to be beaten up. Again, the defender will not have much chance by using simple defense techniques.

However, if the defender is a man of equal physical capability as his attacker, then such a reaction would not be in relation to the attack and the defender could expect to be charged for causing (grievous) bodily harm.

Always try to keep clear of conflicts or try to resolve them verbally. Forceful defense techniques should always be used as a last resort.

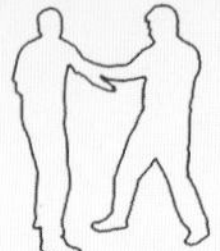

The unwelcome placing of the arms around the waist

1. A is standing on D's left-hand side and has placed his right arm around D's waist.

2. D brings up her left arm to gain momentum...

3. ...and delivers a hammering left-fisted punch into A's genitals.

4. D raises the thumb of the left hand and...

5. ...brings the arm up sharply jabbing the left thumb into A's right eye.

6. D brings her left arm around the back of A's neck...

7. ...and with the right hand she takes A by the throat (larynx) and using this stranglehold brings A down to the ground; this is very dangerous for A because twisting the larynx can cause death.

8. A downward kick ends the combination.

Strangleholds

Strangleholds constitute some of the most dangerous ways of an attack. You can be unconscious within 5 seconds. Therefore using this type of attack is in a life threatening situation and you must be able to react quickly. Assume that you will not be strong enough to free yourself from a stranglehold. Subsequently, you should concentrate on your defense techniques.

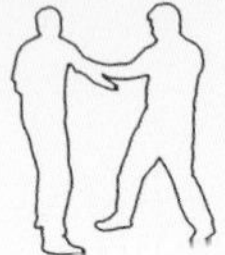

The frontal stranglehold with both hands

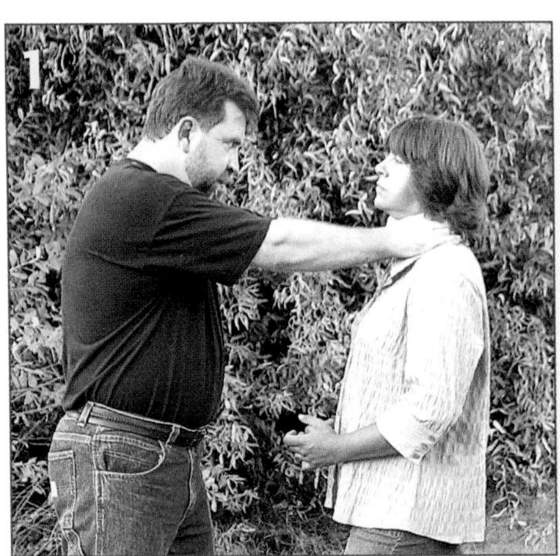

1. A is standing in front of D and is applying a stranglehold with both hands. This is very dangerous for D as within 5 seconds D can become unconscious.

2. D delivers a punch at A's larynx (absolutely dangerous for A!)...

3. ...and brings her hands and arms up through the hold freeing herself.

4. D rubs both of her thumbs over A's eyes...

5. ...grabs hold of the back of A's head in both hands...

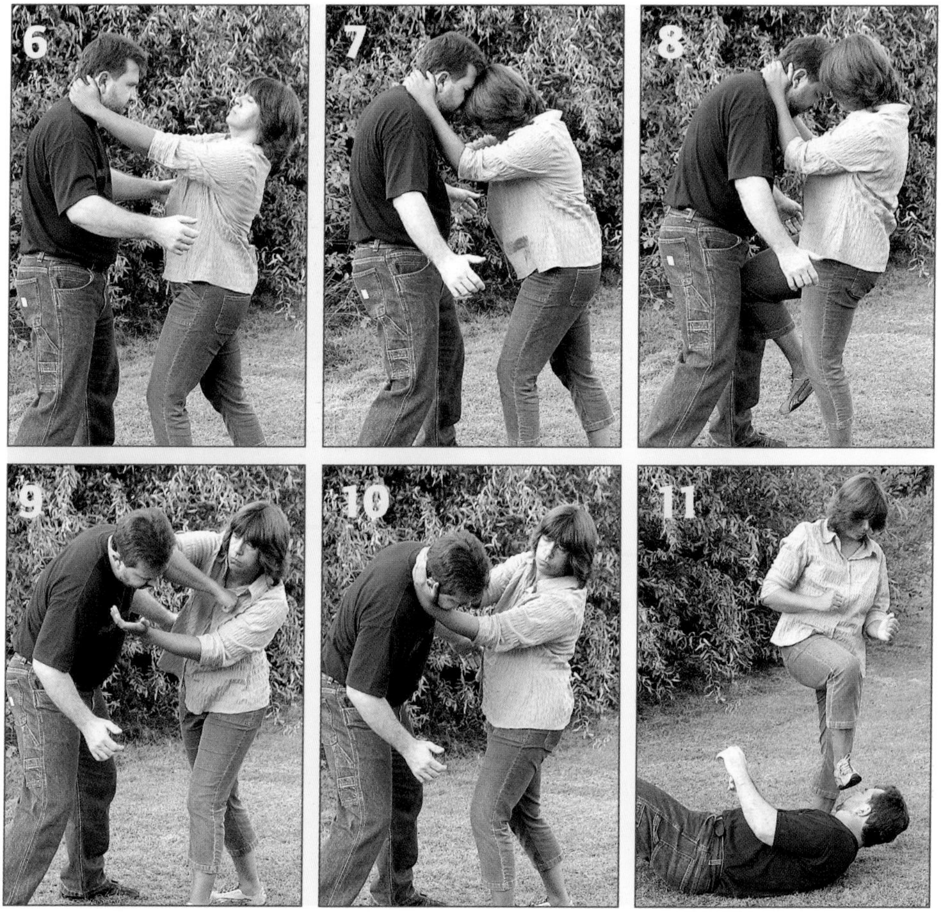

6. ...brings back her head to gain momentum...

7. ...and does a head butt at A's head.

8. D does a knee-up kick at A's genitals...

9. ...followed by a strike with the right elbow at A's head.

10. D then grabs hold of A's head in both hands and twists it to the left bringing him to the ground.

11. A stamping kick downwards at A's head ends the combination.

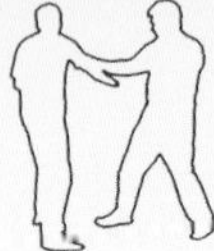

The stranglehold from behind with both hands

1. A is standing behind D and is strangling her with both hands. In this position, D is in great danger of life and within 5 seconds, could lose consciousness, so she must react quickly.
2. D lifts her shoulders up to make the stranglehold more difficult to enforce, and lifts her right hand...
3. ...and brings it down in a hammer punch at A's genitals.
4. D pushes her right arm up vertically (like putting up your hand in school)...
5. ...turns herself clockwise to the right to face A, thus freeing herself of the stranglehold.
6. D delivers a left-fisted punch at A's head...
7. ...then a right-fisted punch at the head...

8. ...followed by a further left-fisted punch at the head (chain blows).

9. D runs her thumbs over A's eyes...

10. ...grabs A's neck in both hands...

11. ...and does a head butt at A's head.

12. D does a right-legged knee-up into A's genitals...

13. ...and a strike with the right elbow at A's head.

14. D grabs hold of the back of A's neck in both hands and twists the head to the left down to the ground...

15. ...ending the combination by stamping downwards on A's head.

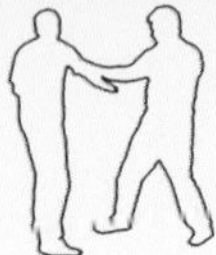

The stranglehold from behind by the use of the forearms

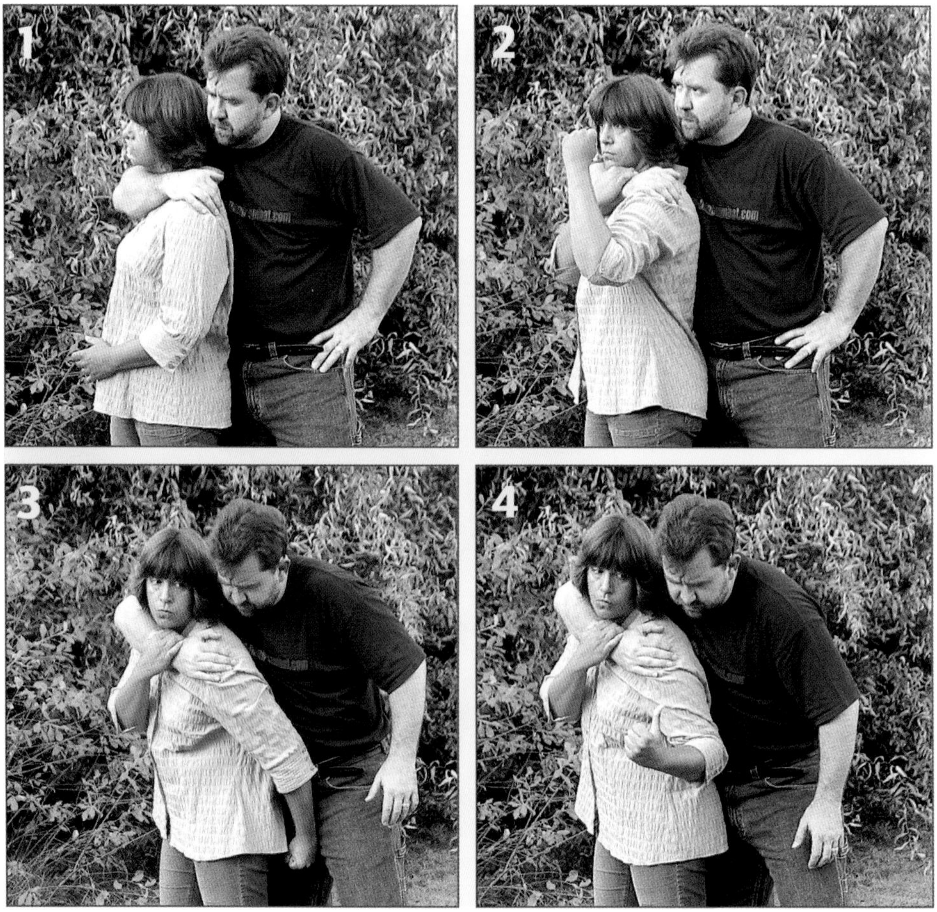

1. A is standing behind D and is strangling her with the right lower arm around her neck. This position is amongst the most dangerous because a counter to it is very difficult. As with all strangleholds, within 5 seconds D could lose consciousness, so she must react quickly.
2. D grabs hold of A's right wrist with the right hand and where possible pulls A's arm downwards. At the same time D lifts her left hand up quickly ...
3. ...and brings a hammer punch down into A's genitals.
4. D then sticks out the left thumb...

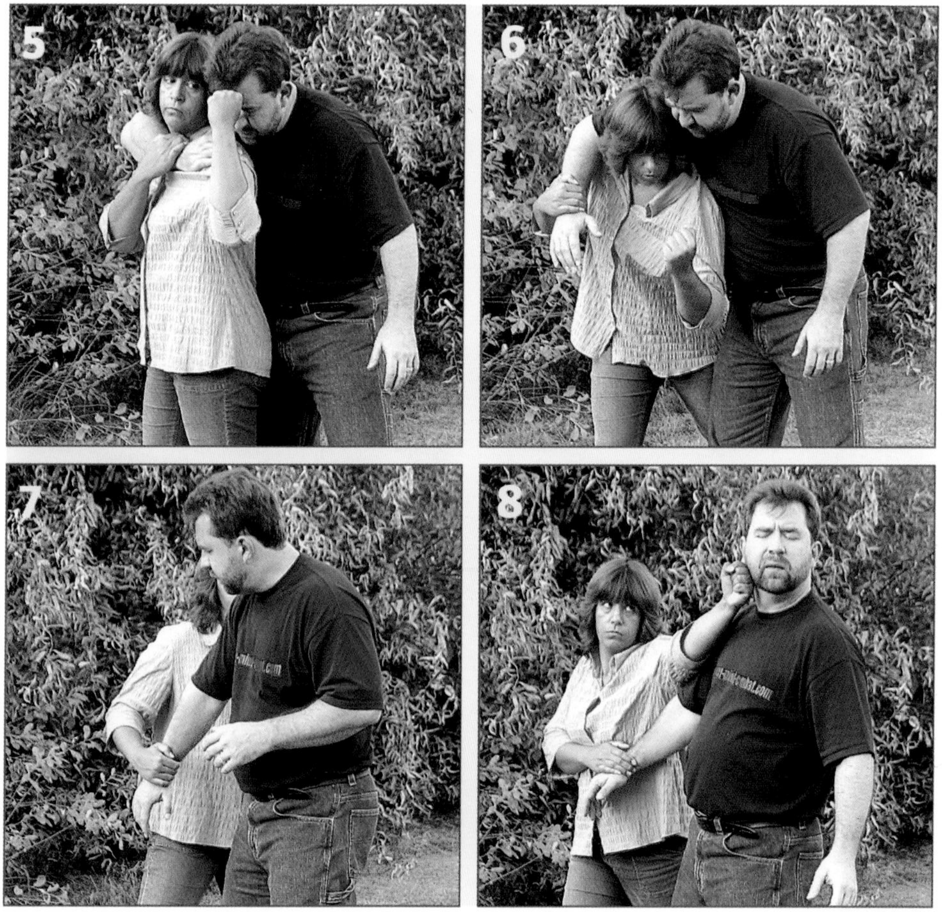

5. ...and jabs it into A's left eye.

6. D pulls A's right arm forcefully downwards...

7. ...ducks through under A's right arm...

8. ...and moves out to the right. This is followed by D delivering a left-fisted punch to A's head.

For those interested in learning more on "Self-defense groundwork", may I recommend my book "Grappling – Effective Groundwork" (Meyer & Meyer 2005), because the subject can only be touched on here in this book.

The attacker is on the ground and is sitting in the guard position

1. A is in between D's legs.
2. D jabs A's eyes with the fingers (disrupting technique)...
3. ...brings the right shin up in front of A's stomach, places the left leg directly alongside A's right leg and does a scissor movement with the legs complementing this by doing a twisting movement with the arms.
4. Once D has turned A over on the back, D delivers a punch at A's nose.

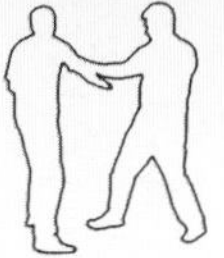

The attacker is on the ground and is sitting on the defender's stomach in the mount position

1. A is sitting on D in the mount position.
2. D punches into A's genitals with the right fist...
3. ...pins A's right arm against her own upper body using the left arm and holds A's right elbow so that the arm cannot be pulled free.
4. D thrusts the hips up violently..
5. ...and twists A over the left shoulder onto the back.
6. D finalizes the combination by delivering a right-fisted punch at A's nose.

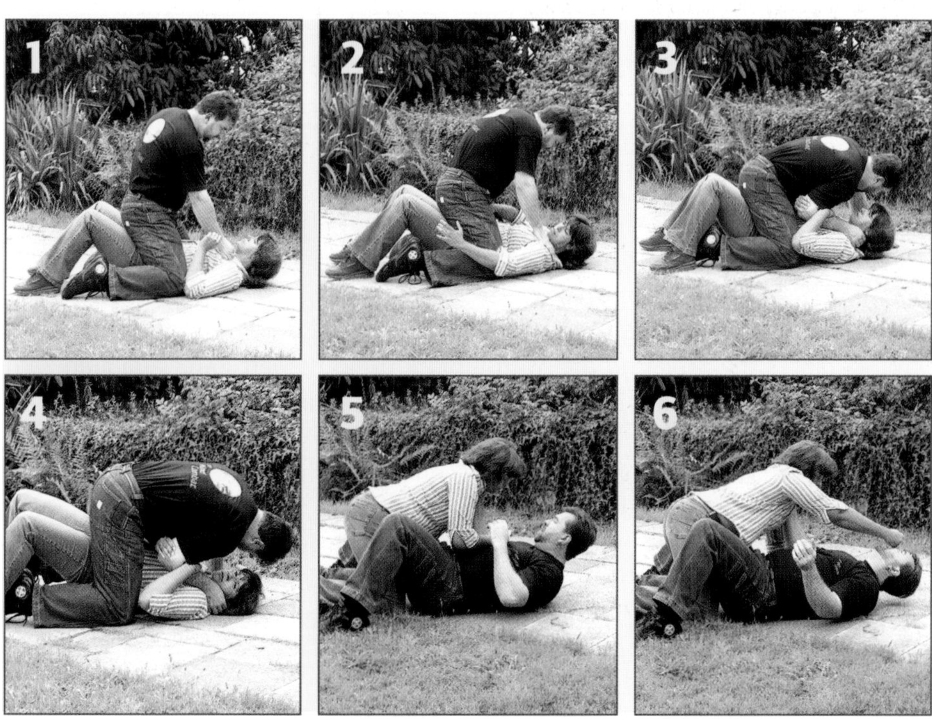

10.2 Attacks with no contact

These types of attacks are done principally by men against men.

An in-swinging punch

1. A delivers an in-swinging punch with the right fist at D's head.
2. D blocks the attacking arm with a block using the left lower arm (Tan Sao), takes a step forward to the right and at the same time delivers a right-fisted punch at A's head.
3. D grabs hold of the back of A's neck with his left hand and delivers a strike at A's head using his right elbow...
4. ...extends his right arm out and places the right hand on the right-hand side of A's head...
5. ...takes hold of A's right arm and places it in twisted arm lock...
6. ...kneeing up at A's head.

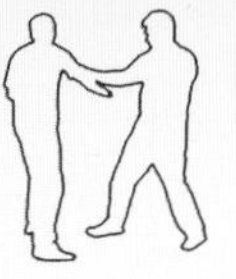

7. D pushes A's right arm upwards with his left hand, pushes A's head clockwise inwards with his right hand...

8. ...and, as he does this, he places his left elbow into A's mouth...

9-10. ...and throws A down to the ground.

11. A stamping kick down onto A's head ends the combination.

An uppercut

1. A delivers a right-fisted uppercut punch at D's head.
2. D blocks it downwards and outwards and at the same time delivers a punch at A's head.
3. With the right elbow D strikes upwards at A's chin...
4. ...straightens his right hand outwards and pushes A's head to the right...
5. ...while delivering a left-fisted punch at A's chin.
6. The combination is ended with a kick at the genitals.

A downward (hammer) punch

1. A delivers a right-fisted hammer punch down onto D's head.
2. D sweeps the punch further downwards...
3. ...and at the same time delivers a right-fisted punch at A's head.
4. With the right elbow D strikes upwards at A's chin...
5. ...straightens his right hand outwards and pushes A's head to the right...
6. ...while delivering a left-fisted punch at A's chin.
7. The combination is ended with a kick at the genitals.

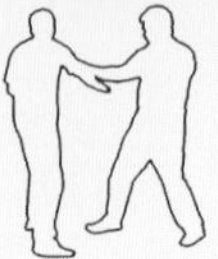

A backhanded punch

1. Standing with his right leg forward, A delivers a right-fisted backhand punch at the right-hand side of D's head.

2. D strikes at the attacking arm with his left elbow and grabs hold of A's attacking arm with his right hand around about the area of the wrist.

3. D places the left lower arm on A's right arm...

4. ...and sweeps it clockwise further downwards to the left...

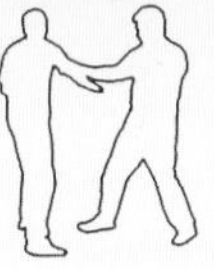

5. ...and at the same time delivers a punch at A's nose...
6. ...followed by a punch at the genitals.
7. D places the right foot behind A's right foot, and pushes his leg against A's leg...
8. ...using this leg lever to bring A backwards down onto the ground.
9. The combination is ended with a kick downwards at A's ankle.

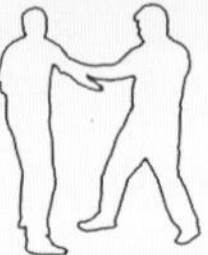

Kicking forwards

1. A kicks D in the genitals with his right leg.

2. D angles his left leg sharply and directs the knee at the shinbone of the attacking leg. This technique is very painful for the attacker. As long as D's leg is well angled at the knee, little will happen to it.

3. D delivers a right-fisted punch at A's head...

4. ...another punch at the head with the left fist...

5. ...and a further punch with the right fist at the head (chain blows).

6. D brings both thumbs over A's eyes...

7. ...grabs around the back of A's head with both hands...

8. ...and does a head butt at A's head.

9. As he straightens himself up, D does a knee-up kick at the genitals...

10. ...followed by a strike with the right elbow at A's head...

11. ...grabs around the back of A's head with both hands...

12. ...and brings A down to the ground by applying pressure to the neck...

13. ...ending the combination with a downward right-foot kick at A's head.

The foot punch forwards

1. A kicks forward with the right foot at D's stomach. D lifts his right leg up...

2. ...and blocks it with his right leg. This turns A around.

3. D places his right leg behind A's right leg...

4. ...from behind, D grabs A's eyes and pulls A's head backwards...

5. ...throwing him to the ground after causing him to bend over backwards.

6. The combination is ended with a downward kick at the head.

The foot punch to the rear

1. A kicks back to the rear with the right foot at D's stomach.
2. D counters this by pushing with his right leg and foot against A's right thigh from behind thus preventing A carrying out the kick.
3. D kicks at A's genitals with his left leg...
4. ...from behind, D grabs A's eyes...
5. ... and pulls A's head back causing him to bend over backwards and fall onto the ground.
6. The combination is ended with a downward kick at the head.

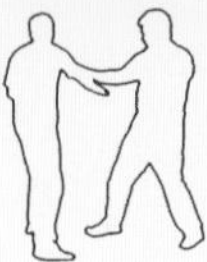

Kneeing up into the genitals

1. A kicks up with his right knee into D's genitals.
2. D carries out a defensive block with his left leg outwards to the left...
3. ...followed by a right-fisted punch at A's head...
4. ...and a further left-fisted punch at the head...
5. ...and finally a right-fisted punch at the head (chain of blows).
6. D brings his thumbs over A's eyes...
7. ...and grabs the nape of A's neck with both hands...

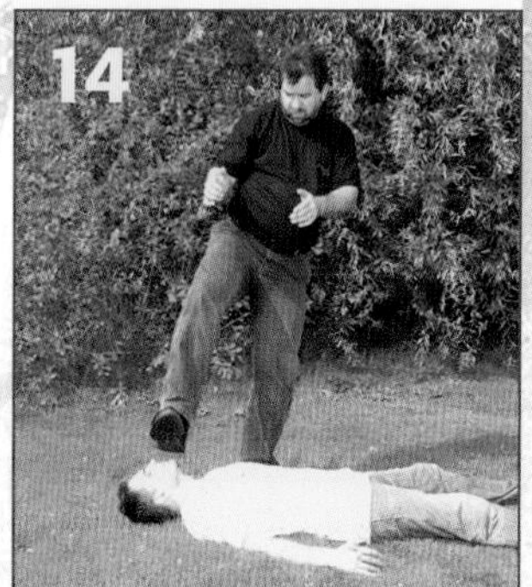

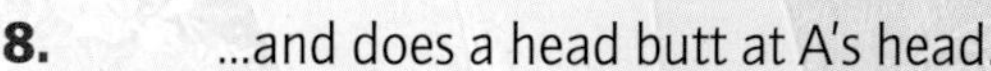

8. ...and does a head butt at A's head.

9. As he lifts himself back up, D does another knee kick into A's genitals...

10. ...followed up by a strike with the right elbow at A's head.

11. D then grabs around the back of A's neck and...

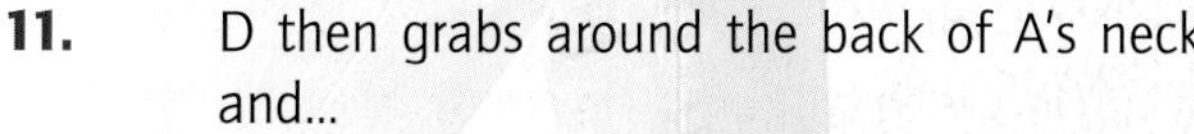

12-13. ...brings A down to the ground by applying pressure on his neck...

14. ...ending the combination by stamping his right foot down on A's head.

The frontal shove

1. A pushes D with both hands.
2. D sweeps the attacking arms downwards and inwards with both hands...
3. ...followed by a right-fisted punch at A's head...
4. ...and a further left-fisted punch at the head...
5. ...and finally a right-fisted punch at the head (chain of blows).
6. D brings his thumbs over A's eyes...

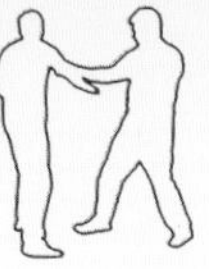

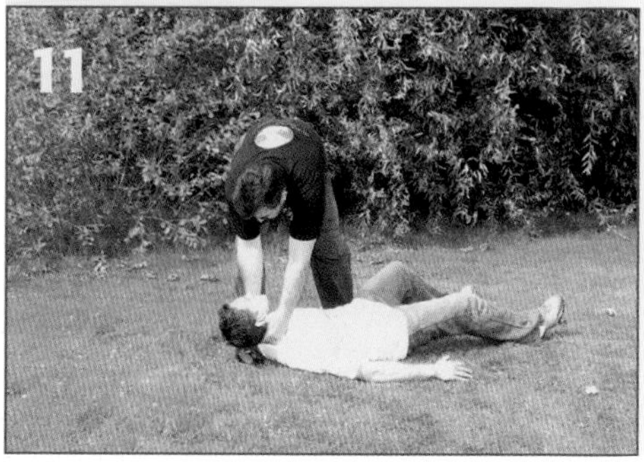

7. ...and grabs the nape of A's neck with both hands and does a head butt at A's head.
8. As he lifts himself back up, D does another knee kick into A's genitals...
9. ...followed up by a strike with the right elbow at A's head.
10. D then grabs around the back of A's neck with both hands and...
11. ...brings A down to the ground by applying pressure on his neck...
12. ...ending the combination by stamping his right foot down on A's head.

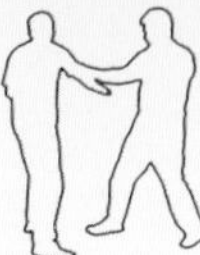

The shove from behind

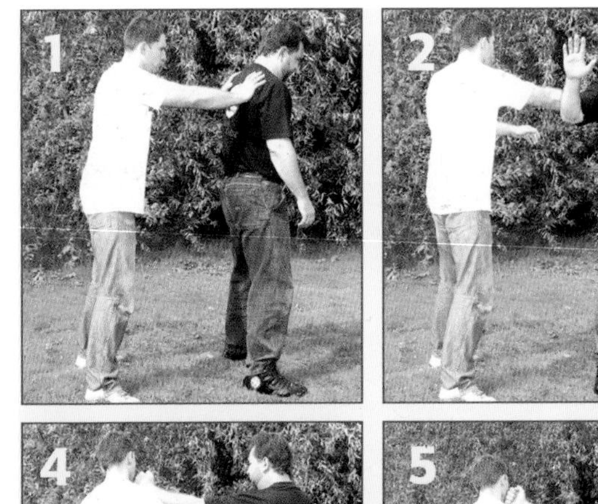

1. A stands behind D and pushes D with both hands.
2. D angles his right arm upwards...
3. ...and twists around pulling his arm backwards rapidly and sweeping A's attacking arms to one side.
4. D delivers a left-fisted punch at A's head...
5. ...and a further right-fisted punch at the head...
6. ...and finally a left-fisted punch at the head (chain of blows).
7. D brings his thumbs over A's eyes...

8. ...and grabs the nape of A's neck with both hands...

9. ...and does a head butt at A's head.

10. As he lifts himself back up, D does another knee kick into A's genitals...

11. ...followed up by a strike with the right elbow at A's head. D then grabs around the back of A's neck with both hands and...

12. ...brings A down to the ground by applying pressure on his neck...

13. ...ending the combination by stamping his right foot down on A's head.

10.3 Special situations

Again, in this section, I assume that the defender is physically weaker than the attacker. The situation is presumed to be that the defender has been attacked. Simple defensive techniques will not be sufficient to avoid a conflict. The defender has tried everything to avoid a fight by talking to the attacker. There is no place to flee to, so it is necessary to use effective defensive techniques.

Please note that in all the combinations the attacker could end up severely injured. For example, applying pressure to the eardrums can lead to a loss of hearing. This could be taken as a case of inflicting grievous bodily harm and there is the danger that the defender ends up prosecuted and serving a possible prison sentence.

Against a dangerous attack, you need to employ effective defense techniques. However, only use these whenever your life is in danger. Do not be provoked by a verbal onslaught.

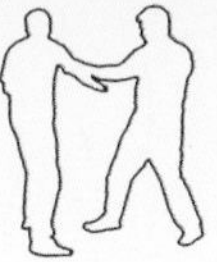

In the bar

1. D is standing at the bar. A approaches him from the right-hand side, lays his left hand on D's right shoulder and grabs hold of D's drink with his right hand.

2. D grabs hold of A's right wrist with his right hand so that A cannot lift the glass.

3. D pushes his right leg between A's legs and places his foot behind the heel of A's right foot.

4. D pulls A's right leg forward...

5. ...and strikes backwards at A's head with his right elbow.

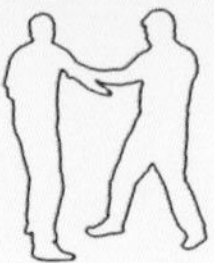

1. D is standing at the bar. A approaches him from the right-hand side and stands beside D.
2. D lays his right hand on A's left shoulder to prevent him delivering a punch at the head...
3. ...and at the same time carries out a kick with the right knee at A's right knee so that A is pushed back against the bar.
4. Then D strikes down on A's nose with his right fist...
5. ...and then punches him in the genitals with the right fist.

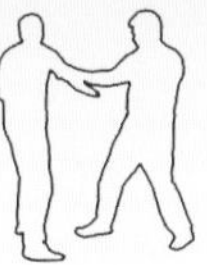

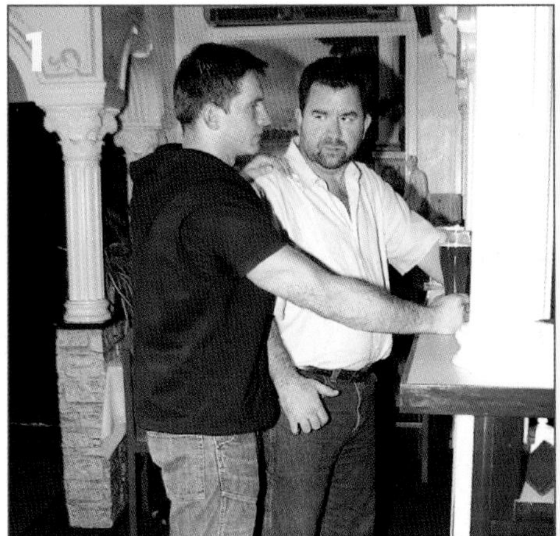

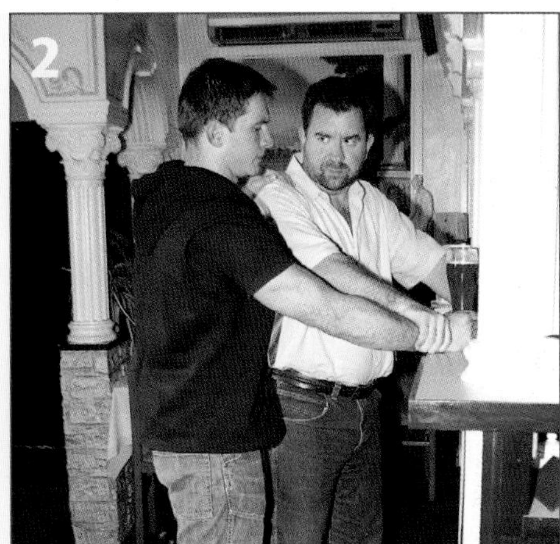

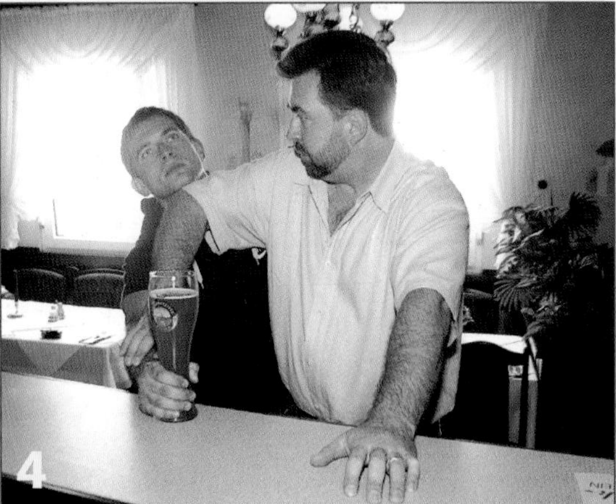

1. D is standing at the bar. A approaches him from the right-hand side and stands just behind D. A then lays his left hand on D's right shoulder and grabs hold of D's drink with his right hand.

2. D grabs hold of A's right wrist with his right hand so that A cannot lift the glass.

3. D kicks his right foot down A's left shin and sweeps A's left leg to the rear...

4. ...and brings his right elbow upwards against A's chin.

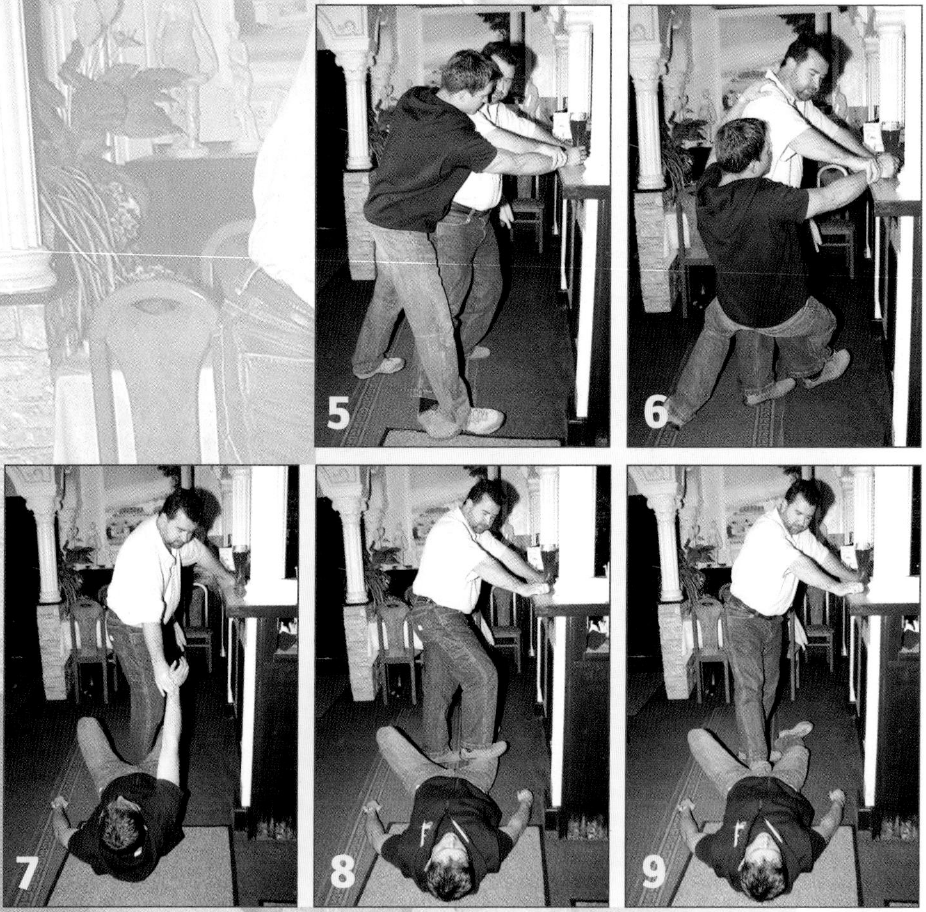

5. D now places his right foot directly behind A's right foot...

6. ...and pushes the whole of his upper body to the right against A's body so that A loses his balance backwards (D still keeps hold of A's right hand).

7. D sweeps A's right leg forwards with his own right foot so that A falls over backwards and has to sit down.

8. D now does a stamping kick with his right leg downwards at A's right knee. D could also jump on A's right knee with both legs, but this would certainly cause a broken leg.

9. D places his right foot on A's genital area to end the combination.

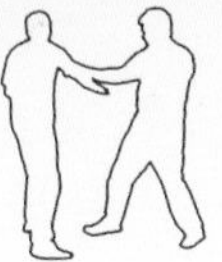

In the bar sitting at a table

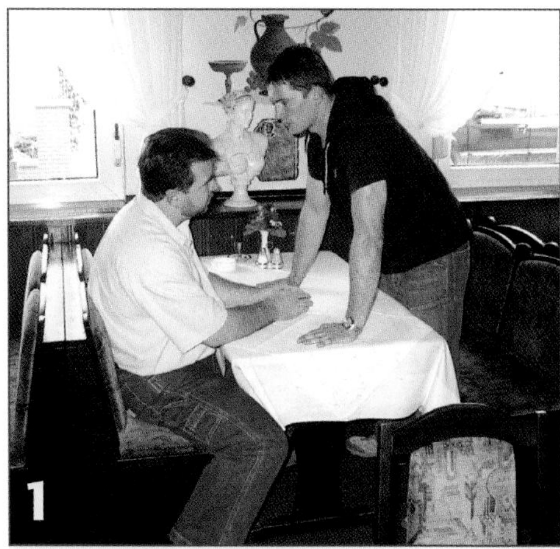

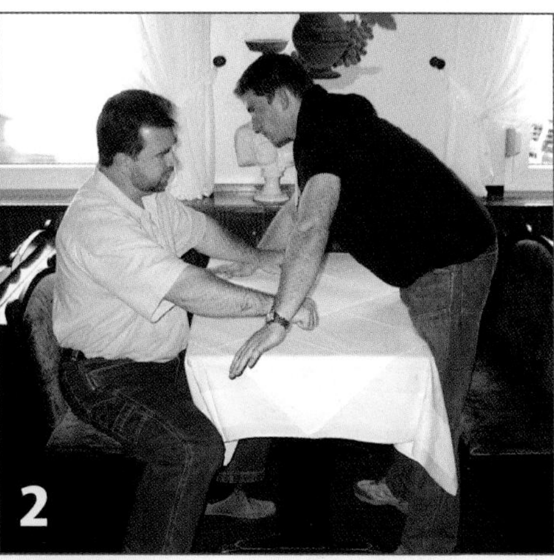

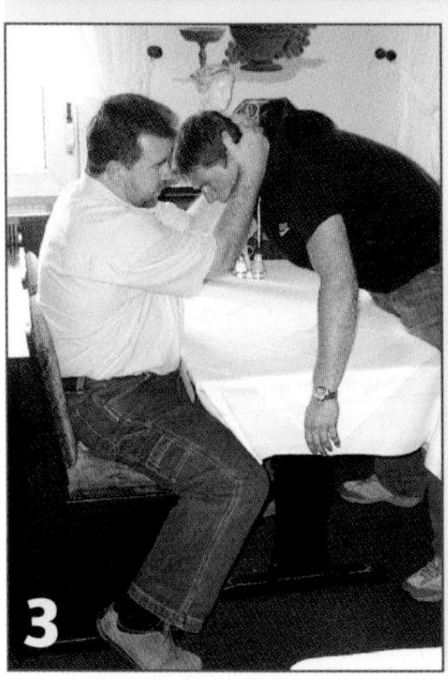

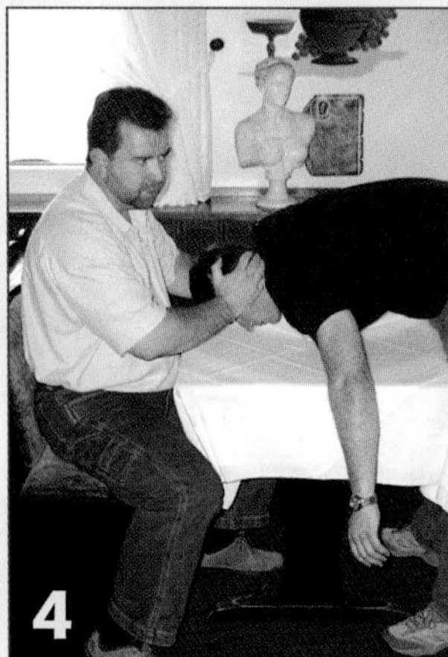

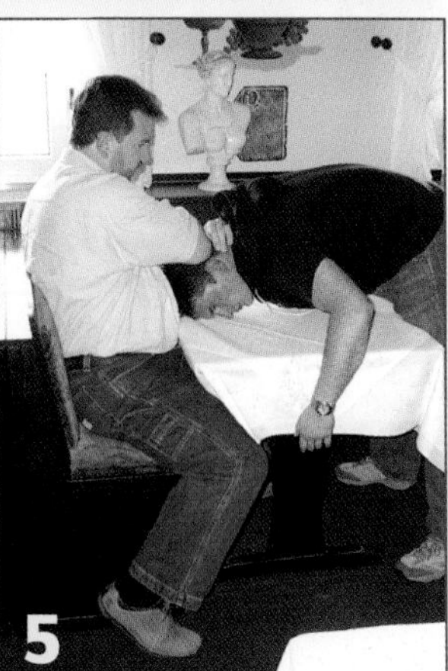

1. D is sitting at a table and A looms over him placing both hands on the table in front of D and leans towards him.
2. D sweeps both arms outwards so that A falls onto the table with his chest...
3. ...and D grabs hold of A's nape of the neck with both hands...
4. ...and smashes A's head down against the table.
5. A strike forwards with the right elbow at A's head ends the combination.

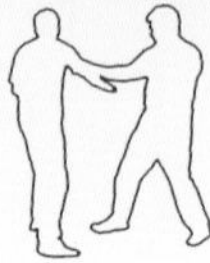

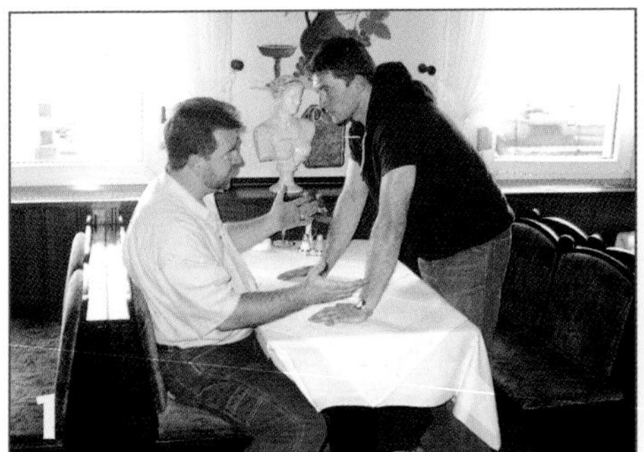

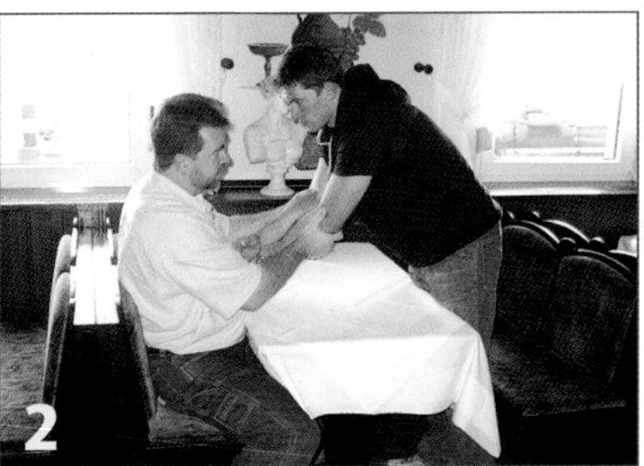

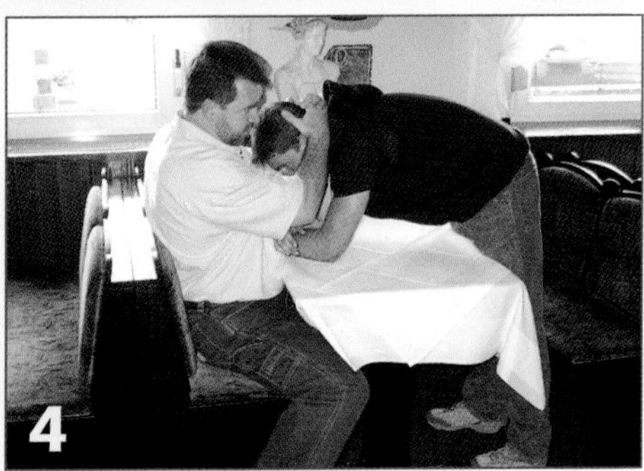

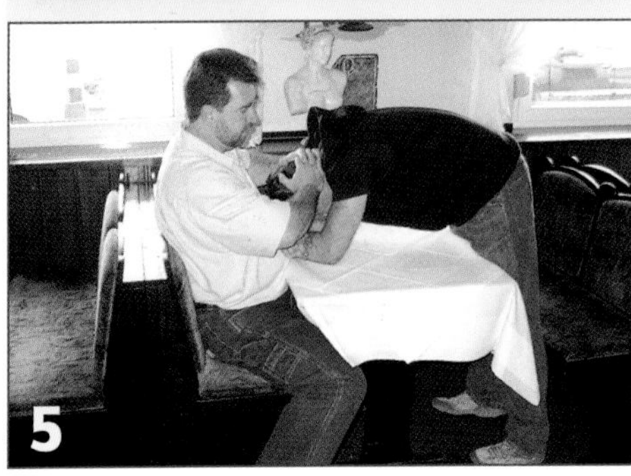

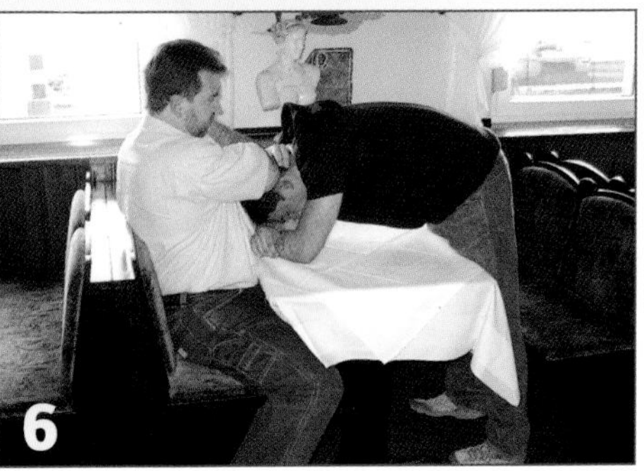

1. D is sitting at a table and A looms over him placing both hands on the table in front of D and leans heavily towards him. D lifts both hands up around the outside of A's arms...
2. ...and slaps with both palms of the hands against A's elbows...
3. ...bringing A's arms together.
4. ...and D grabs hold of A's nape of the neck with both hands...
5. ...and smashes A's head down against the table.
6. A strike with the right elbow at A's head ends the combination.

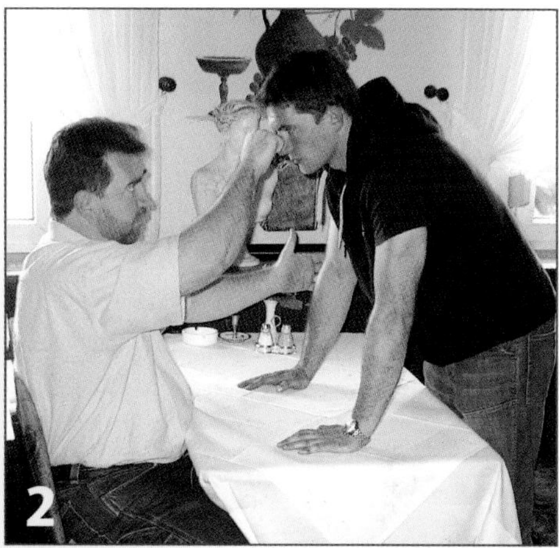
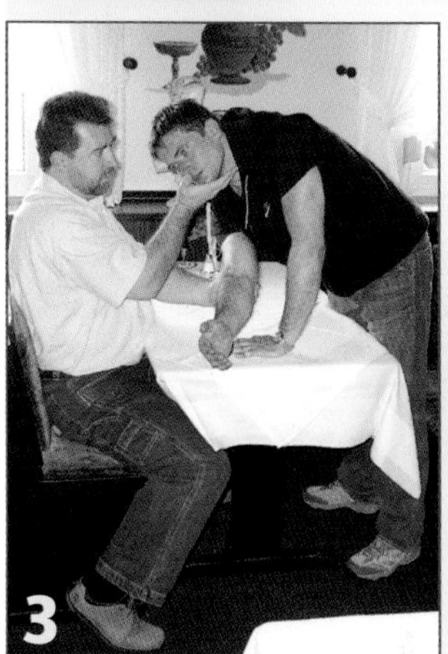
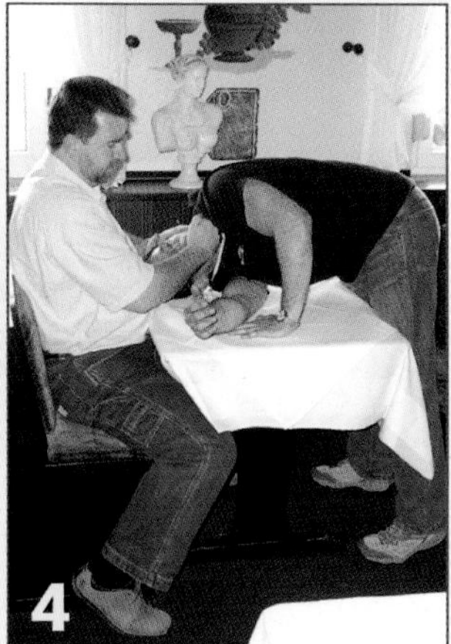
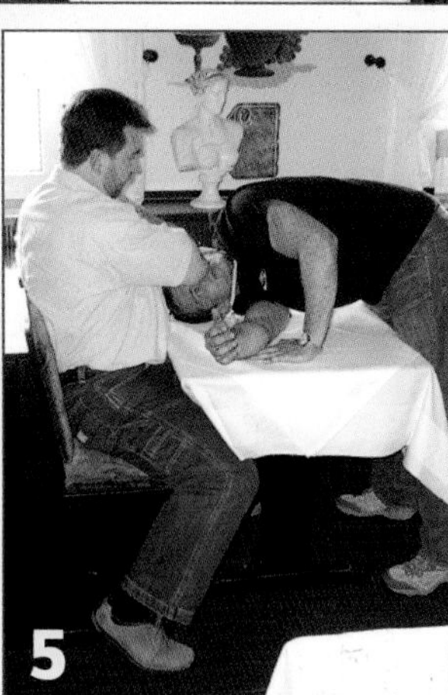

1. D is sitting at a table and A looms over him placing both hands on the table in front of D and leans heavily towards him.

2. D does a right-fisted knuckle punch at A's nose...

3. ...and with his left hand sweeps A's right arm inwards to the right and places the right hand on the right-hand side of A's head...

4. ...and smashes the back of A's head onto the table.

5. D strikes forwards with the right elbow at A's head ending the combination.

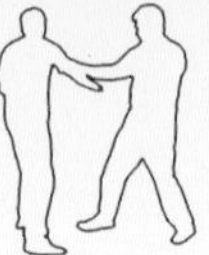

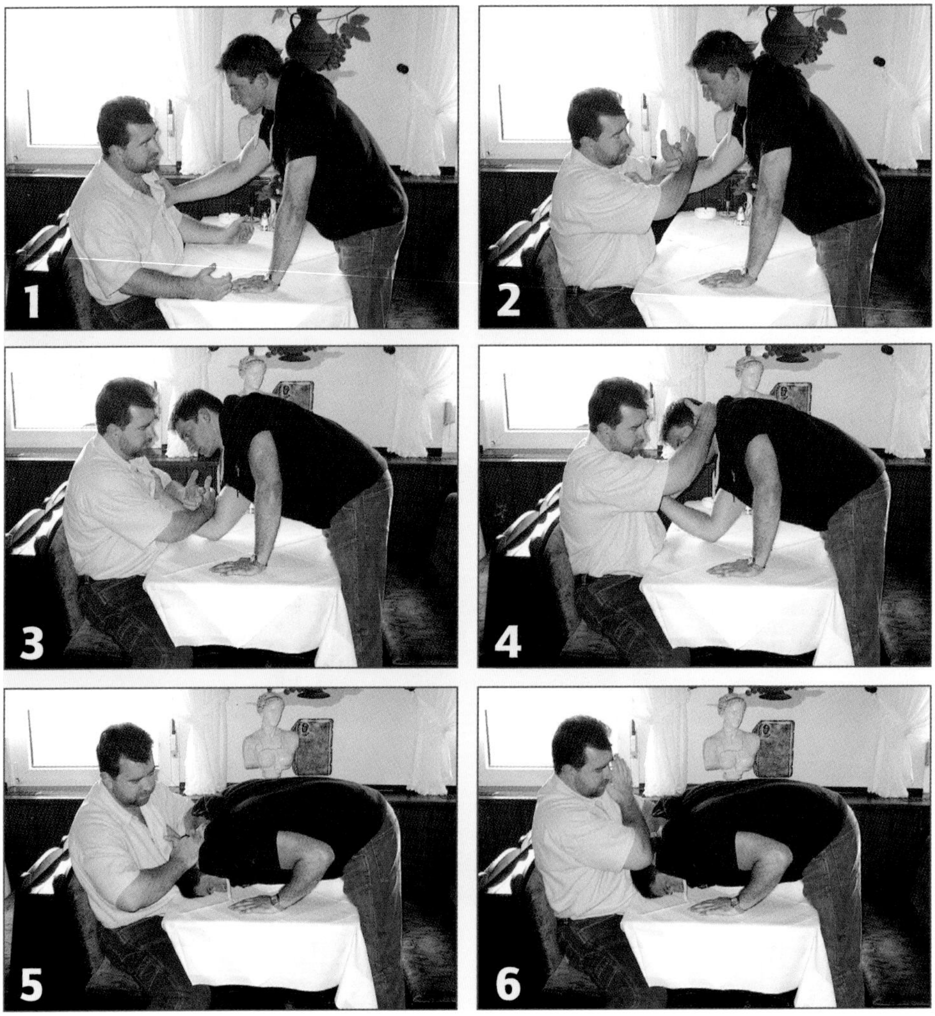

1. D is sitting at a table and A looms over him and with his right hand grabs hold of D's T-shirt. A leans heavily towards D.
2. D brings both of his arms over A's right arm and places the edges of the hands on A's right lower arm...
3. ...and pushes A's right arm forcibly down on to the table.
4. D grabs hold of the back of A's head...
5. ...and smashes A's head onto the table.
6. D strikes forwards with the right elbow at A's head ending the combination.

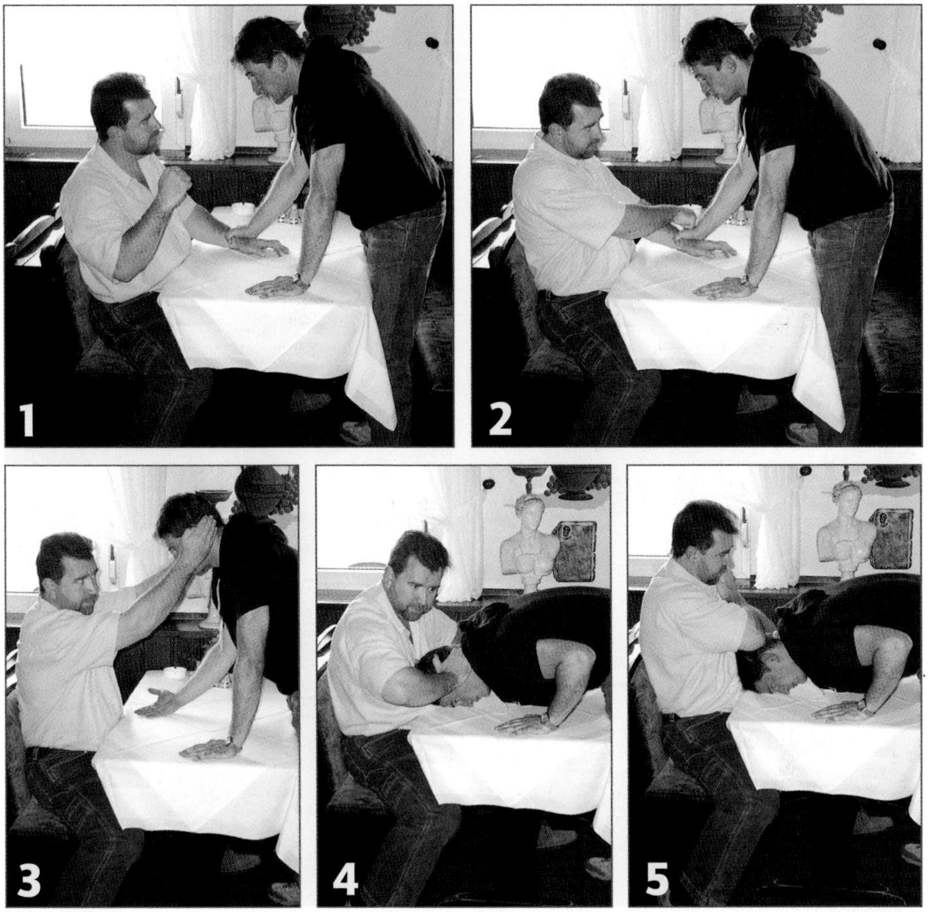

1. D is sitting at a table and A looms over him and grabs hold of D's left wrist with his right hand. A leans heavily towards D.
2. D does a right-fisted knuckle punch at the back of A's right hand. There is a nerve point here and this causes A to release his grip.
3. D slaps A's ears with both hands, and grabs around behind A's neck...
4. ...and smashes A's head onto the table.
5. D strikes forwards with the right elbow at A's head ending the combination.

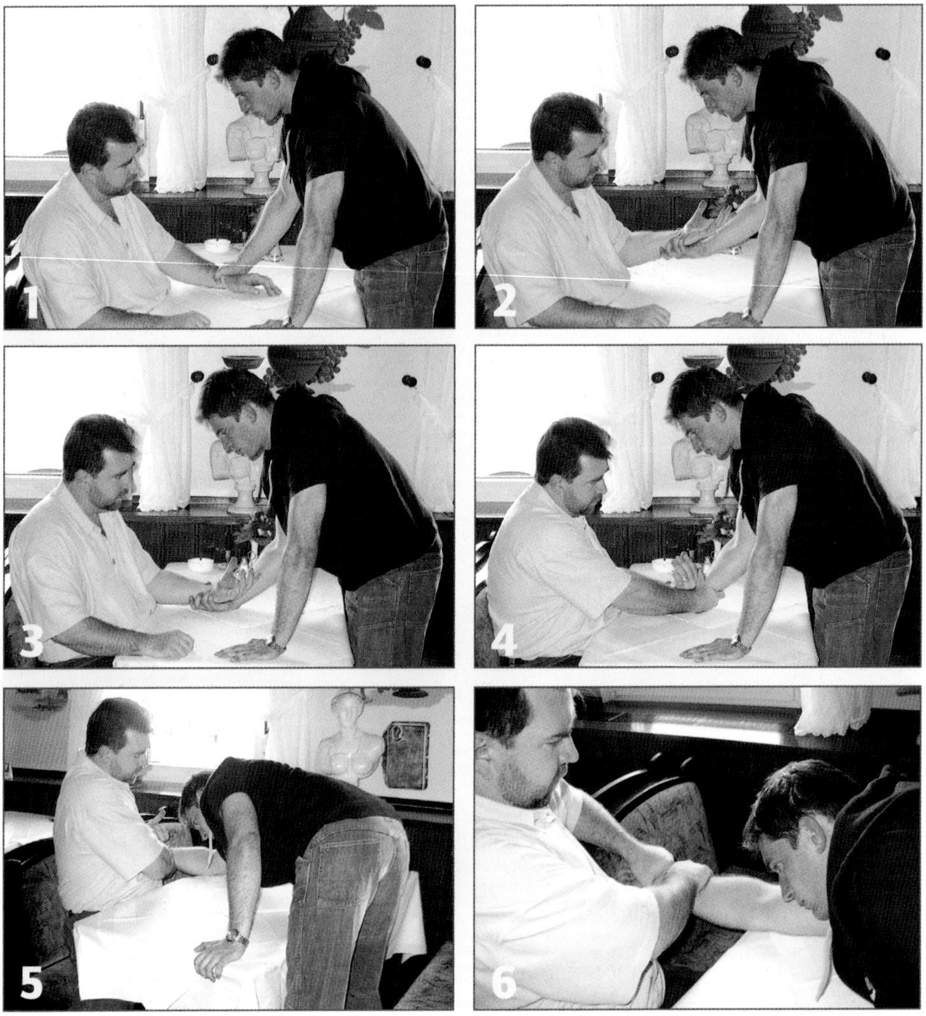

1. D is sitting at a table and A looms over him and grabs hold of D's left wrist with his right hand. A leans heavily towards D.
2. D lifts his left hand up...
3. ...and turns it over so that the palm of A's hand is pointing up at the ceiling.
4. D grabs hold of A's right wrist with his right hand...
5. ...and with both hands pulls A's arm over the edge of the table until A's elbow is on the edge of the table...
6. ...and stretches (breaks) A's arm downwards over the edge of the table.

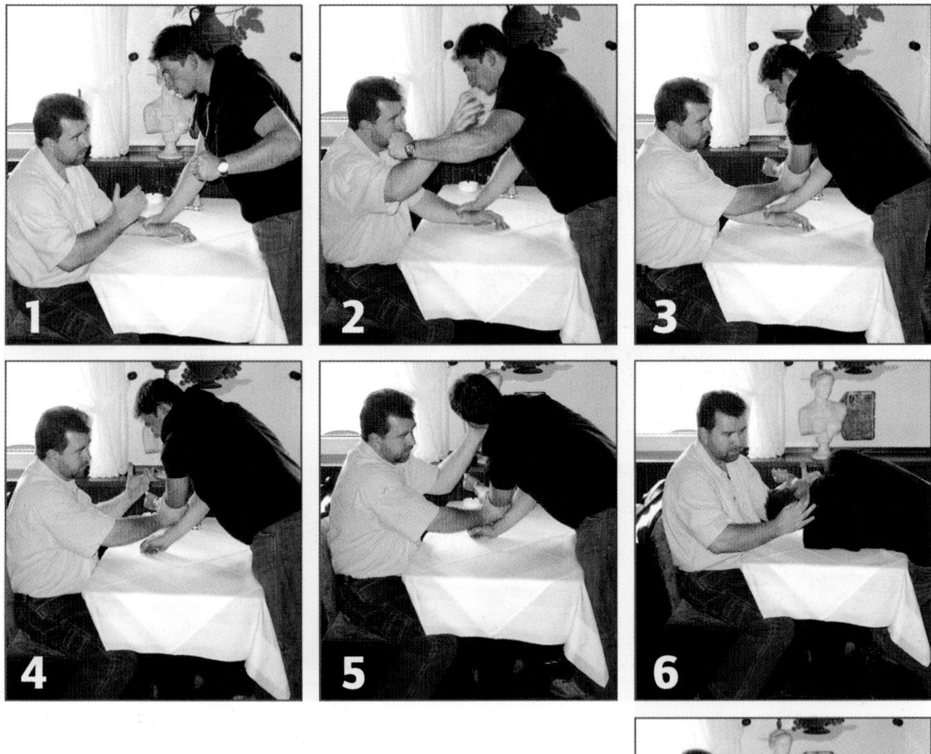

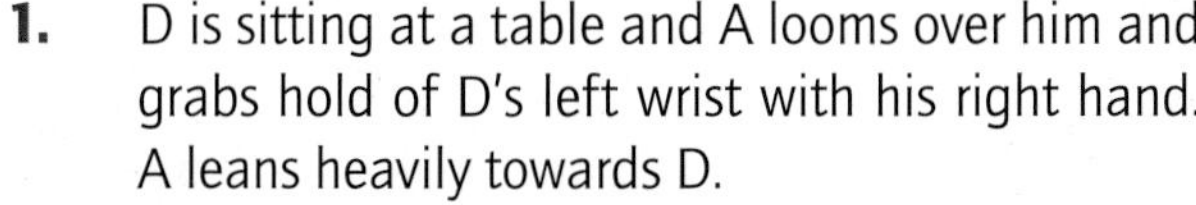

1. D is sitting at a table and A looms over him and grabs hold of D's left wrist with his right hand. A leans heavily towards D.

2. A delivers an in-swinging punch with his left fist at D's head. D blocks this outwards to the right with his lower arm...

3. ... and brings A's left arm down onto the table...

4. ...freeing the grip with his left hand.

5. D then grabs A's chin in his left hand...

6. ...and brings A's head using a neck lock lever onto the table.

7. D strikes forward with the right elbow at A's head ending the combination.

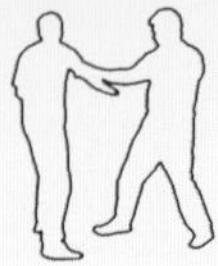

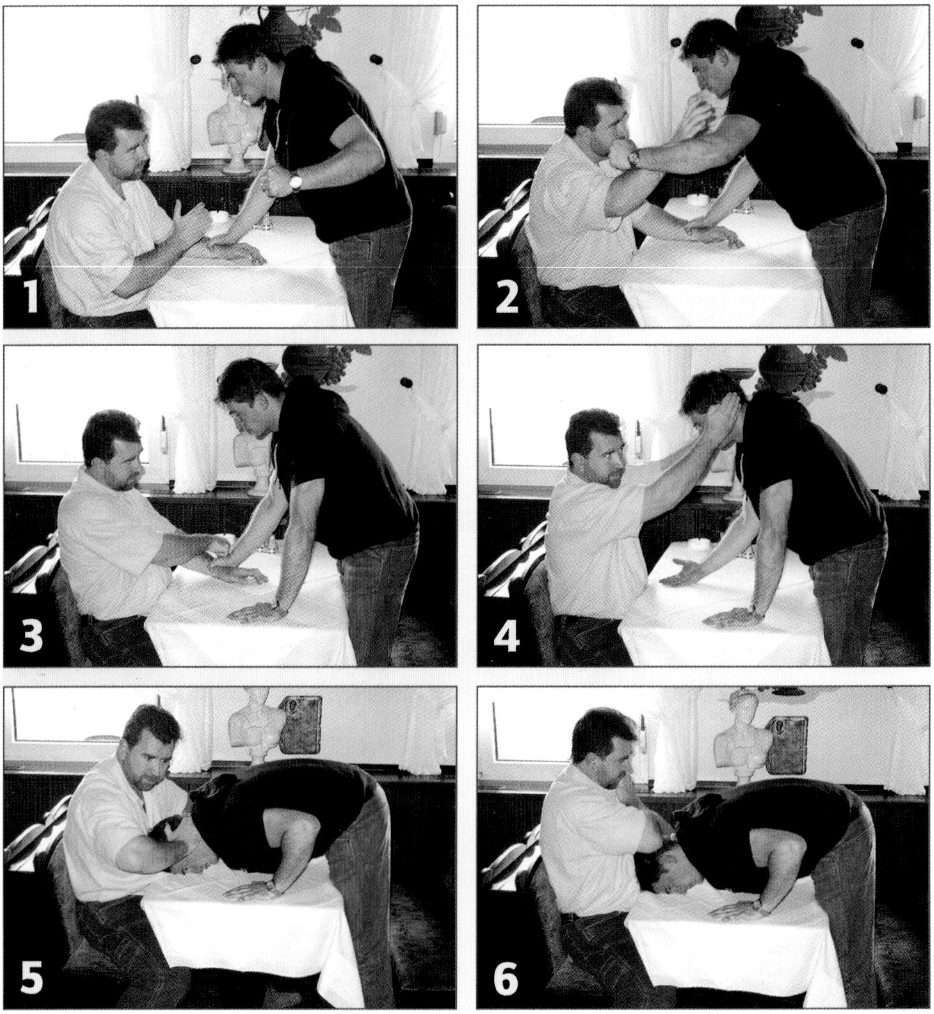

1. D is sitting at a table and A looms over him and grabs hold of D's left wrist with his right hand. A leans heavily towards D.
2. A delivers an in-swinging punch with his left fist at D's head.
3. D does a knuckle punch at the back of A's right hand. There is a nerve point here and this causes A to release his grip.
4. D slaps A's ears with both hands, and grabs around behind A's neck with both hands...
5. ...and smashes A's head onto the table.
6. D strikes forwards with the right elbow at A's head ending the combination.

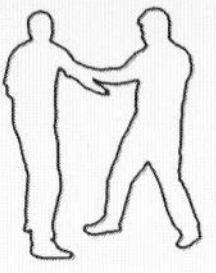

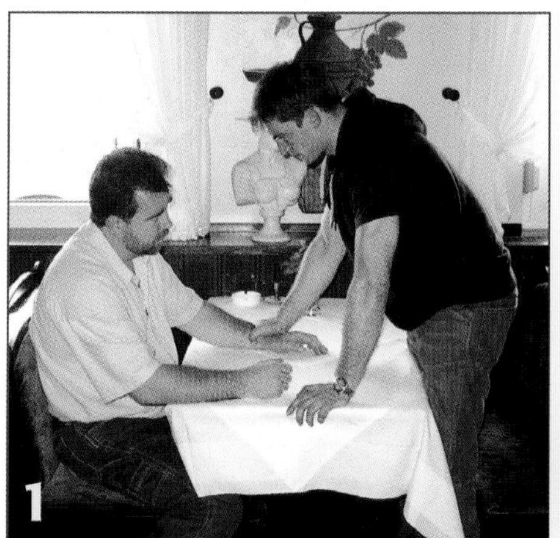

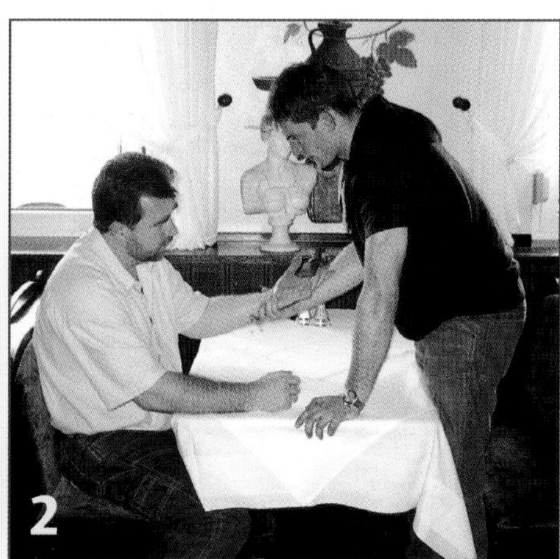

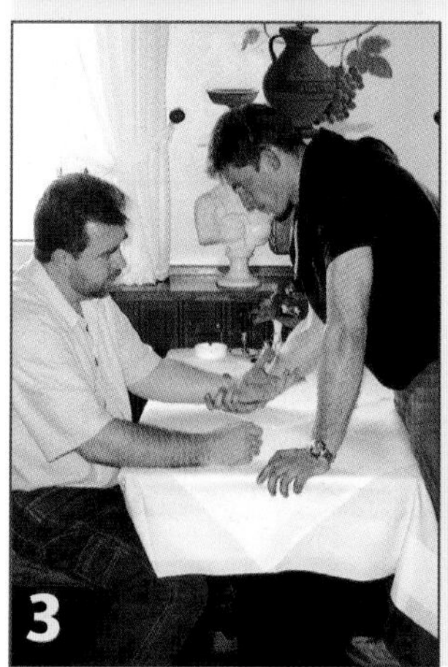

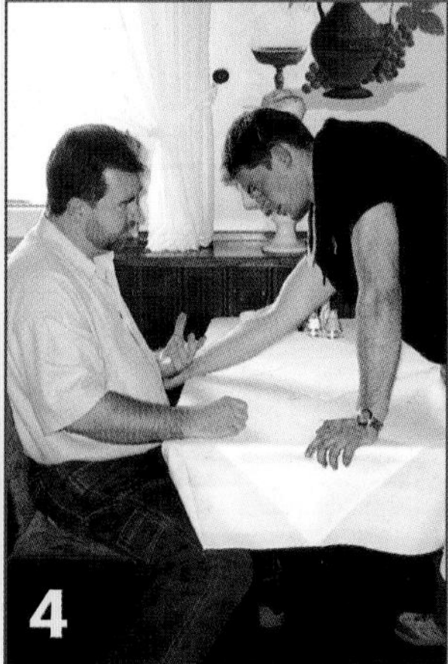

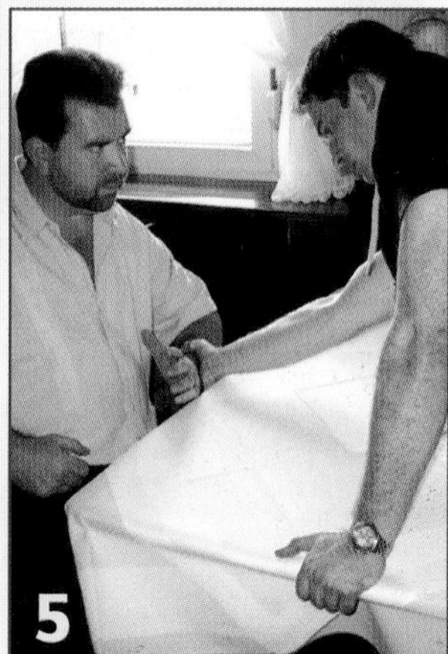

1. D is sitting at a table and A looms over him and grabs hold of D's left wrist with his right hand. A leans heavily towards D.
2. D lifts his left arm up and turns it over...
3. ...and smashes A's right hand down onto the table...
4. ...and then pulls A's right hand across and over the edge of the table...
5. ...and pushes the hand down under the edge of the table.

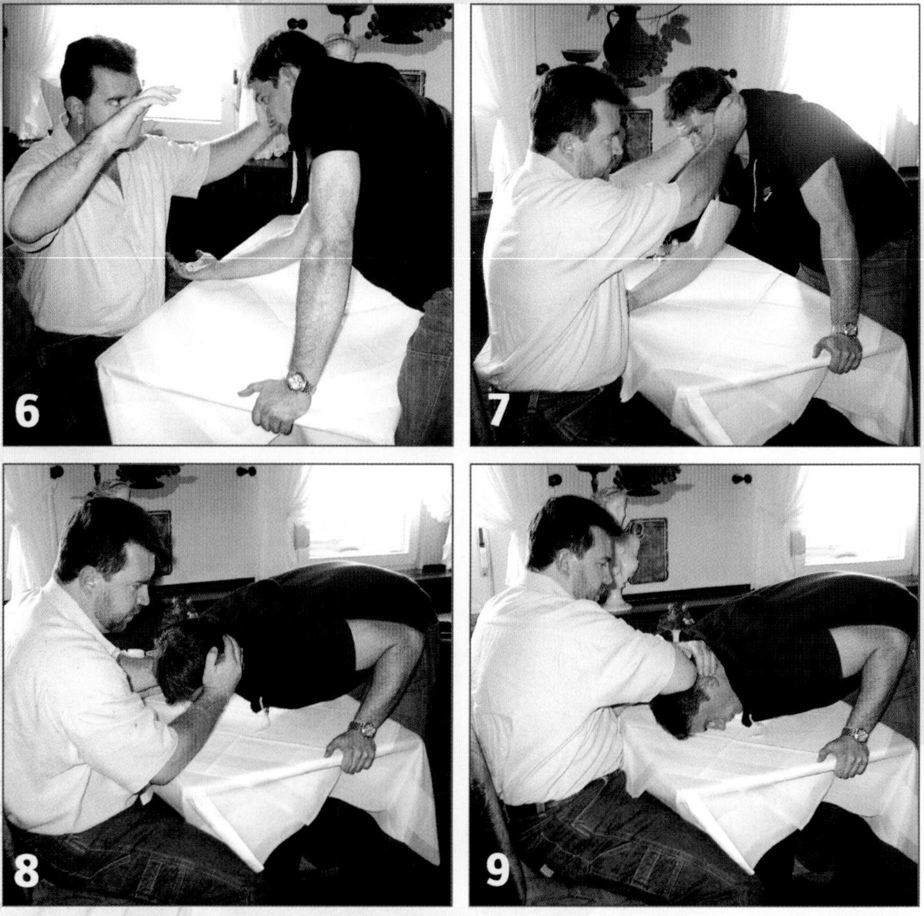

6. D brings both arms up to gain momentum...

7. ...and slaps his hands over A's ears to create pressure...

8. ...and brings A's head down on to the table...

9. ...ending the combination with a strike of the right elbow at A's head.

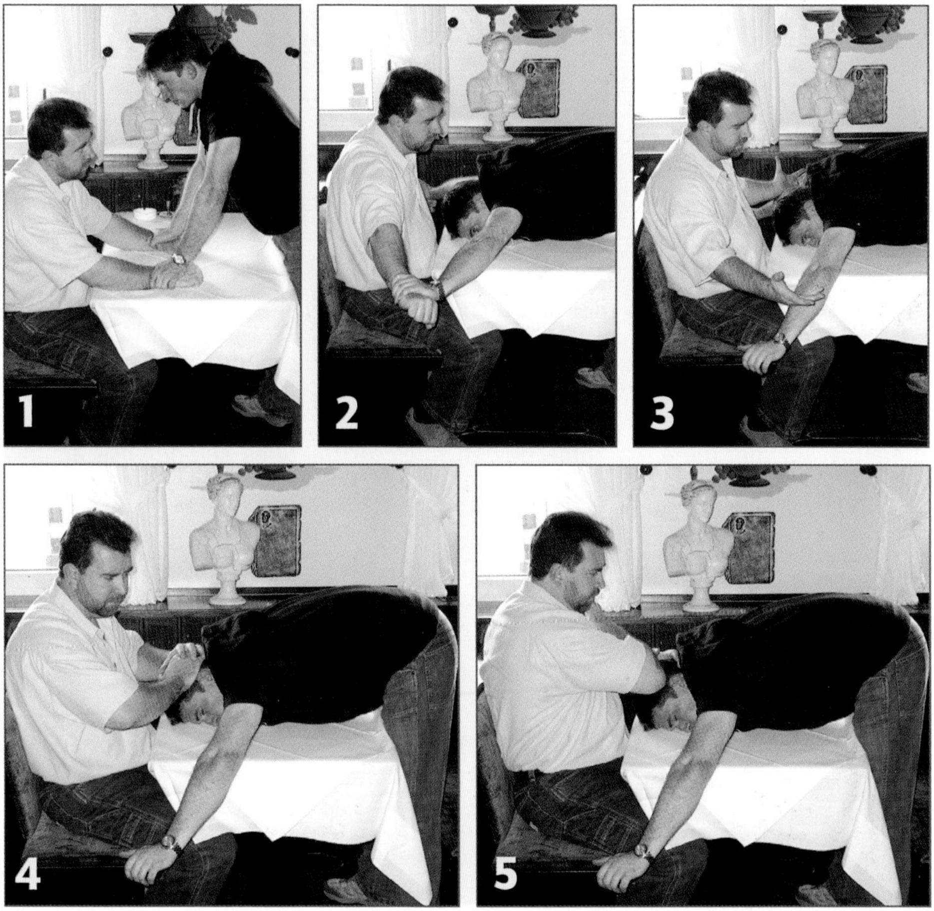

1 2 3 4 5

1. D is sitting at a table and A looms over him and grabs hold of both of D's wrists with both hands. A leans heavily towards D.

2. D brings both arms outwards rapidly so that A's collapses with his head onto the table.

3. D frees both of his hands using a freeing technique...

4. ...grabs around the back of A's head with both hands and bangs A's head down onto the table several times.

5. D ends the combination with a strike of the right elbow forwards at A's head.

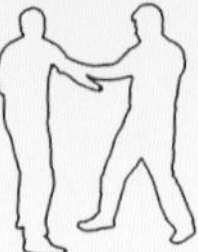

11 Unarmed Self-Defense Against Knife Attacks

For those interested, may I refer you to my book *"Self-Defense Against Knife Attacks"* (Meyer & Meyer 2006) for more details, because it is only possible to touch on such an expansive theme here in this book.

Several studies have shown that unarmed defense against someone trained to use a knife can never end up without injuries being inflicted – even though the attacker is up to 6 m away from you before he attacks!

Therefore, for me, there are three golden rules for unarmed self-defense against knife attacks:

- Get the hell out of it!
- Get the hell out of it!
- Get the hell out of it!

In this case, running away is not cowardly, it's actually rather clever!

Unfortunately, it is not always possible to run away, therefore I want to show the options here that increase the probability of surviving a knife attack. However, the defender should be prepared, right from the beginning, that he will be injured by the knife. It's now about limiting this injury to a minimum.

In the following, the reader will be made aware of the different possibilities for defense against a knife attack. For this, first of all, the natural human reflexes will be used and concepts for effective defense presented. Techniques demanding coordination follow in the secondary step. Drills are used in order to sharpen up the movement sequences. Finally, although possibly injured, a way is shown how one can survive the attack of an expert. Techniques for the different distances: long-distance, short-distance, and for groundwork are also demonstrated.

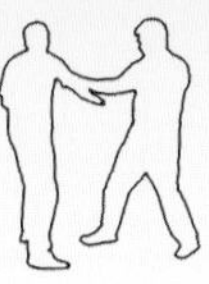

11.1 The basics

In principle, at the very first suspicion of a knife attack the defender should cover his throat with his hands, so that a surprise attack will injure the hands and not the throat. To do this, the back of the hands should point towards the attacker, because a cut on the back of the hands is not as dangerous as a cut on the inside of the forearm.

Besides that, the defender should attempt, if possible, to place something between him and the attacker and therefore gain more time to be able to react. After the successful defense, the defender should get away as quickly as possible and notify the police.

When there are things available that one can use as objects to attack with or to keep one's distance with (e.g. a chair, stick...), the defender should use them. He can also take off his belt and use the buckle to strike back with, or wind his jacket around his arm and use this arm as a shield. He could also take off his shoes, put these over his hands, and ward off the attacker with them.

If the knife has not yet been drawn, but the attacker makes it clear that a knife attack is imminent, then the defender can react against the attacker and, for example, stab him in the eyes with the fingers since the attack was about to take place and would be a criminal act, thus allowing you to use the rule of self-defense.

11.2 Ways of holding the knife

Generally, I assume here that two knife positions can be used: the dagger/ice pick position (the blade is on the side where the little finger is) and the normal knife position (the blade is on the side where the thumb is). There are other variations besides these two positions, but I do not want to discuss these in further detail here.

1

2

11.3 Attack angles

According to many of the systems that address themselves to self-defense against knife attacks, the first five angles of attack are identical. These and others will be presented in the following lessons. Essentially, Attack Angles 1-5 will be the ones covered in this book.

For the Angles 1-4, it doesn't matter if the knife is in the normal knife or dagger position. For Angle 5 it does make a difference. When the knife is held in the knife position (blade is on the thumb side), it is possible to strike and also stab.

As a rule, all attacks should not only be executed with the right hand, but also with the left. This applies for all combinations and exercises described in this book.

11.3.1 Angle No. 1 (Knife strike/stab coming in downwards and inwards from the outside at the neck)

The strike/stab is carried out from the right downward and inwards from the outside at the left side of D's neck.

11.3.2 Angle No. 2 (Knife strike/stab coming in downwards and outwards from the inside at the neck)

The strike/stab is carried out from the left downwards and outwards from the inside at the right side of D's neck.

11.3.3 Angle No. 3 (Knife strike/stab from the outside inwards at waist level)

The strike/stab is carried out from the right at hip height horizontally at the left side of D's upper body (hip height).

11.3.4 Angle No. 4 (Knife strike/stab from the inside towards the outside at waist level)

The strike/stab is carried out from the left at hip height horizontally at the right side of D's upper body (hip height).

11.3.5 Angle No. 5 (Knife stab at the stomach)

Normal knife position: The stab is carried out directly at D's stomach.

Dagger position: The stab is carried out vertically downwards at D's head/upper body.

11.4 Defense against knife attacks and disarming techniques

The first combination for each of the attack angles is as far as possible the same. This has been done deliberately so that there is only one single movement for all of the attack angles.

Examples of disarming techniques can be as follows:

- With the hand
- With the edge of the hand
- With the lower arm
- Over the upper arm
- Over the thigh
- By striking the weapon bearing hand or arm
- Over the attacker's body

- **With the hand**

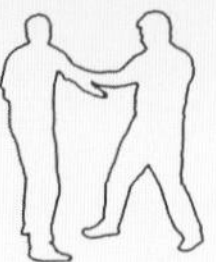

- **With the edge of the hand**

- **With the lower arm**

Example 1

Example 2

- **Over the upper arm**

- **Over the thigh**

- **By striking the weapon bearing hand or arm**

Example 1

Example 2

- **Over the attacker's body**

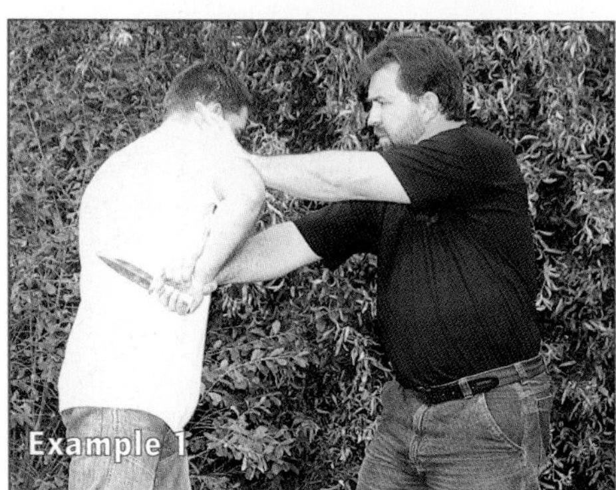

Example 1

Example 2

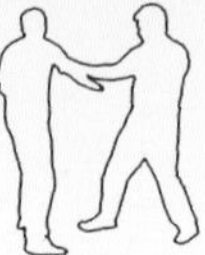

11.4.1 Ways of securing the weapon after a successful disarming

As far as the disarming has been done using the hand, then the defender has hold of the weapon and can use it to defend himself or simply keep hold of it as a piece of evidence. If the weapon falls down to the ground, then it is sensible to pick it up straight away and keep hold of it. In a situation where you are defending yourself and there are several people around then it can be very dangerous to bend down to pick the weapon up. One of these other people could also suddenly attack you. In this case it would be better to place your foot on the weapon. This way it is also safe and cannot be used by anybody else and the defender doesn't run the risk of having to bend down and suffer a surprise attack as he picks it up. The defender should keep the weapon firmly under his foot until the attackers have gone away and it becomes safe to bend down to pick it up.

11.4.2 Defense against a knife attack and disarming techniques

Angle # 1: (Knife thrust at the neck downward from the outside)

1. A strikes with Angle # 1 (downwards and inwards at the neck).

2. D carries out a block with the edge of his left hand upwards and outwards while at the same time delivering a jab at the eyes (disrupting technique) with the fingers of his right hand and taking a 45° step forwards with the right foot...

3. D's right lower arm is placed underneath A's right arm...

4. ...and brings the weapon bearing arm clockwise upwards with the right arm...

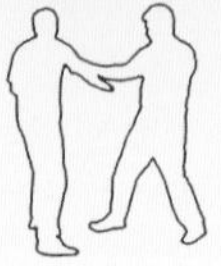

5. ...and then further downwards as he takes a step backwards with his right leg...
6. ...grabbing hold of the ball of the thumb with his right hand...
7. ...and carries out a disarming technique using the left hand (the palm of the left hand is pointing upwards as he does this).
8. Finally, D delivers a kick into A's genitals.

Angle # 2: (Knife thrust at the neck downward from the inside)

1. A strikes with Angle # 2 (downwards from the inside at the neck).

2. D counters by carrying out a block with the edge of his right hand outwards while at the same time delivering a jab at the eyes (disrupting technique) with the fingers of his left hand and taking a 45° step forwards with the left foot...

3. D grabs hold of the ball of the thumb with his right hand...

4. ...and brings the arm clockwise outwards to the left.

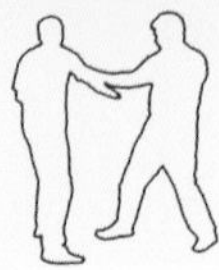

5. D stretches out his left arm (as if he wants to tickle A under his arm)

6. D then places the blunt, flat side of the knife on the left upper arm. D pulls A's right hand over the upper arm with his right hand carrying out the disarming technique over his own body.

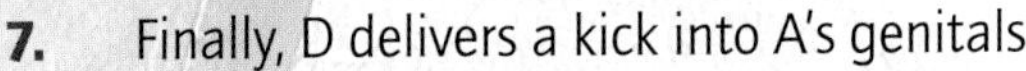

7. Finally, D delivers a kick into A's genitals.

Angle # 3: (Knife thrust at the stomach from the outside)

1. A strikes with Angle # 3 (from the outside at the stomach).
2. With his right arm, D sweeps the knife diagonally downwards while at the same time delivering a jab at the eyes (disrupting technique) with the fingers of his left hand and turning away to the left...
3. ...placing the right hand on A's right lower arm...
4. ...sweeping A's right arm counter-clockwise down to the right and outwards...
5. ...grabbing hold of the ball of A's right thumb with his left hand...

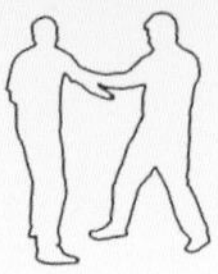

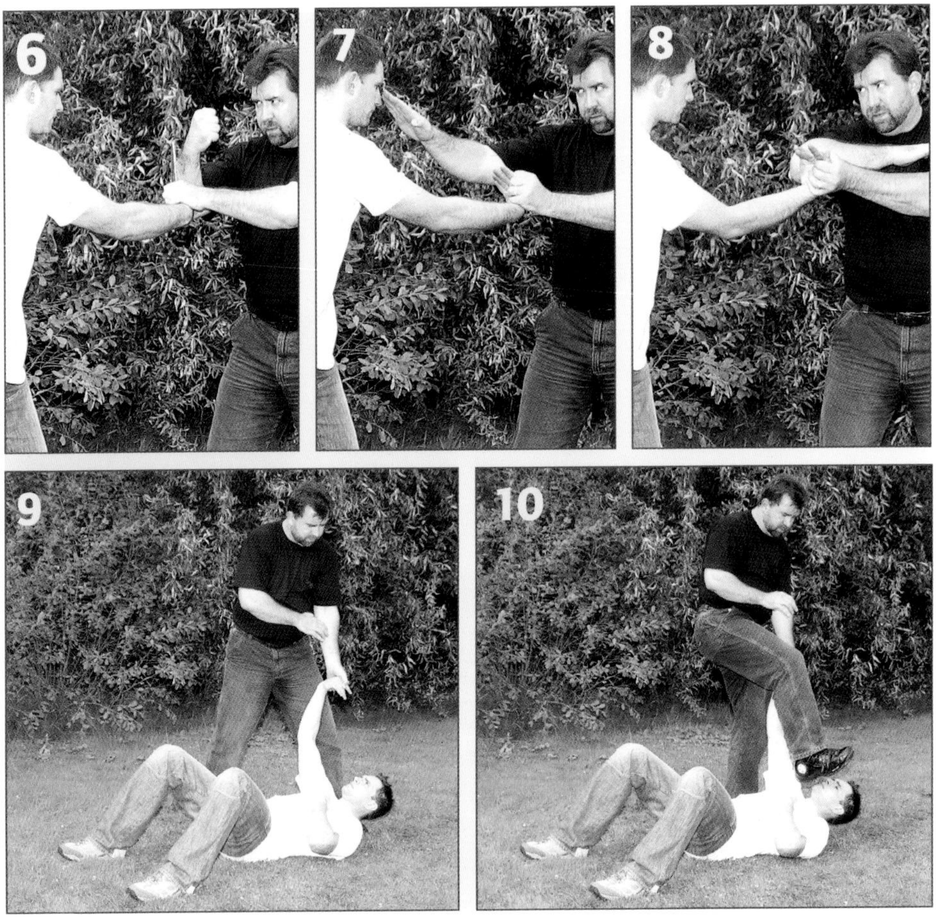

6. ...and places the right lower arm on the blunt side of the knife...

7. ...and carries out a disarming technique using the right lower arm. At the same time D delivers a finger jab at A's eyes with his right hand.

8. D places the right elbow on the back of A's right hand...

9. ...and brings A down to the ground by means of a bent hand lever.

10. D ends the combination by carrying out a stamping kick at A's head with his right foot.

Angle # 4: (Knife thrust at the stomach from the inside)

1. A strikes with Angle # 4 (inwards at the stomach).
2. D carries out a block with the edge of his right hand downwards and outwards while at the same time delivering a jab at the eyes (disrupting technique) with the fingers of his left hand and taking a 45° step forwards with the left foot...
3. D grabs hold of the ball of A's right thumb with his left hand...
4. ...and brings A's right hand counter-clockwise upwards placing the right upper arm on the blunt side of the knife...

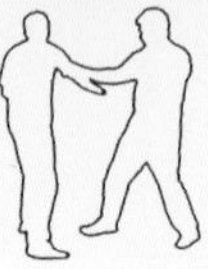

5. ...and carries out a disarming technique using the right lower arm while at the same time delivering a jab at A's eyes with the fingers of the right hand.

6. D delivers a strike with his elbow upwards at A's head...

7. ...pushing A's face outwards to the right...

8. ...and ends the combination with a left-fisted punch.

Angle # 5: (Knife thrust at the stomach)

1. A strikes with Angle # 5 (at the stomach).
2. D carries out a block with the edge of his right hand downwards and outwards while at the same time delivering a jab at the eyes (disrupting technique) with the fingers of his left hand and taking a 45° step forwards with the left foot...
3. ...D grabs hold of the ball of A's right thumb with his left hand...
4. ...and places the edge of the right hand on the blunt side of the knife...
5. ...and carries out a disarming technique using the edge of the hand.
6. D delivers a number of punches beginning with the right fist.
7. This is followed by a punch at A's head with the left fist...

8. ...followed by a further punch at A's head with the right fist.
9. D presses his thumbs over A's eyes...
10. ...and grabs A at the back of the neck with both hands...
11. ...and delivers a head butt at A's head...
12. ...and then a kick at A's genitals with the right knee.
13. D delivers an elbow strike at A's nose...
14. ...pushing A's head with the right hand outwards to the right...
15. ...ending the combination with a left-fisted punch at A's head.

11.5 Knife attacks with close contact

1. A is standing in front of D and has placed his left hand on D's neck. A is holding the knife in front of D's stomach with his right hand.
2. D grabs hold of A's weapon-bearing arm in both hands. For this the left hand is on top of the weapon-bearing arm and the right hand underneath it. At the same time D takes a step 90 to the rear. D twists A's weapon-bearing arm so that A's right elbow is pointing upwards...
3. ...and he pins A's arm in a stretched arm lever.
4. D kicks backwards with his left foot at A's head...
5. ...and places the little finger of the right hand above A's forefinger on the right hand...
6. ...and carries out a disarming technique using the right hand.

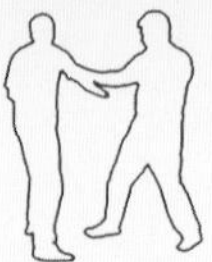

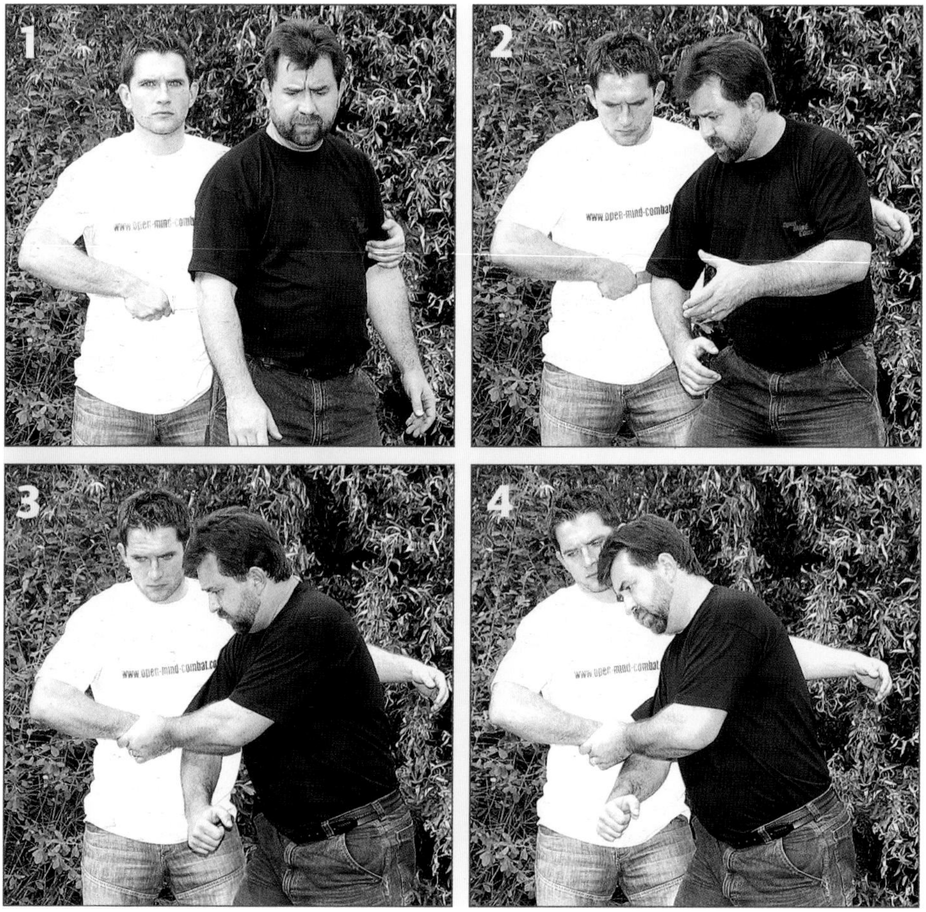

1. A is standing behind D to one side and is holding the knife in his right hand (behind D's right arm) pointing at the kidneys. With his left hand, A grabs hold of D's left arm from behind.

2. D pushes his bent, right arm backwards against the blunt edge of the knife and pushes it with his own upper arm against A's upper body.

3. D grabs hold of A's right wrist with his left hand...

4. ...and does a head butt at A's head...

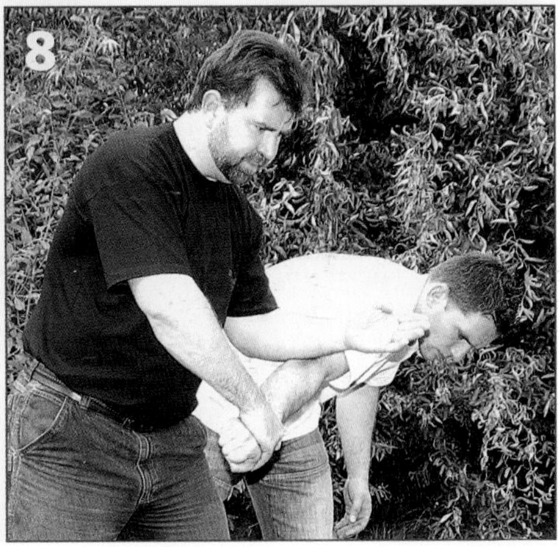

5. ...pulls the knife forwards and as he does disarms A.

6. With his right lower arm, D strikes against A's right elbow joint and effects an arm breaking lock.

7. D brings A's right arm clockwise inwards with both hands...

8. ...places the left lower arm on top of A's right elbow and ends the combination with a stretched arm lock.

1. A is standing behind D to one side and is holding the knife in his right hand (in front of D's right arm) pointing at the liver. With his left hand, A grabs hold of D's left arm from behind.
2. D turns inwards pushing the weapon-bearing wrist firmly against A's stomach.
3. D presses his right lower/upper arm against the blunt edge of the knife and pushes it firmly against A's upper body.
4. D does a head butt at A's head...

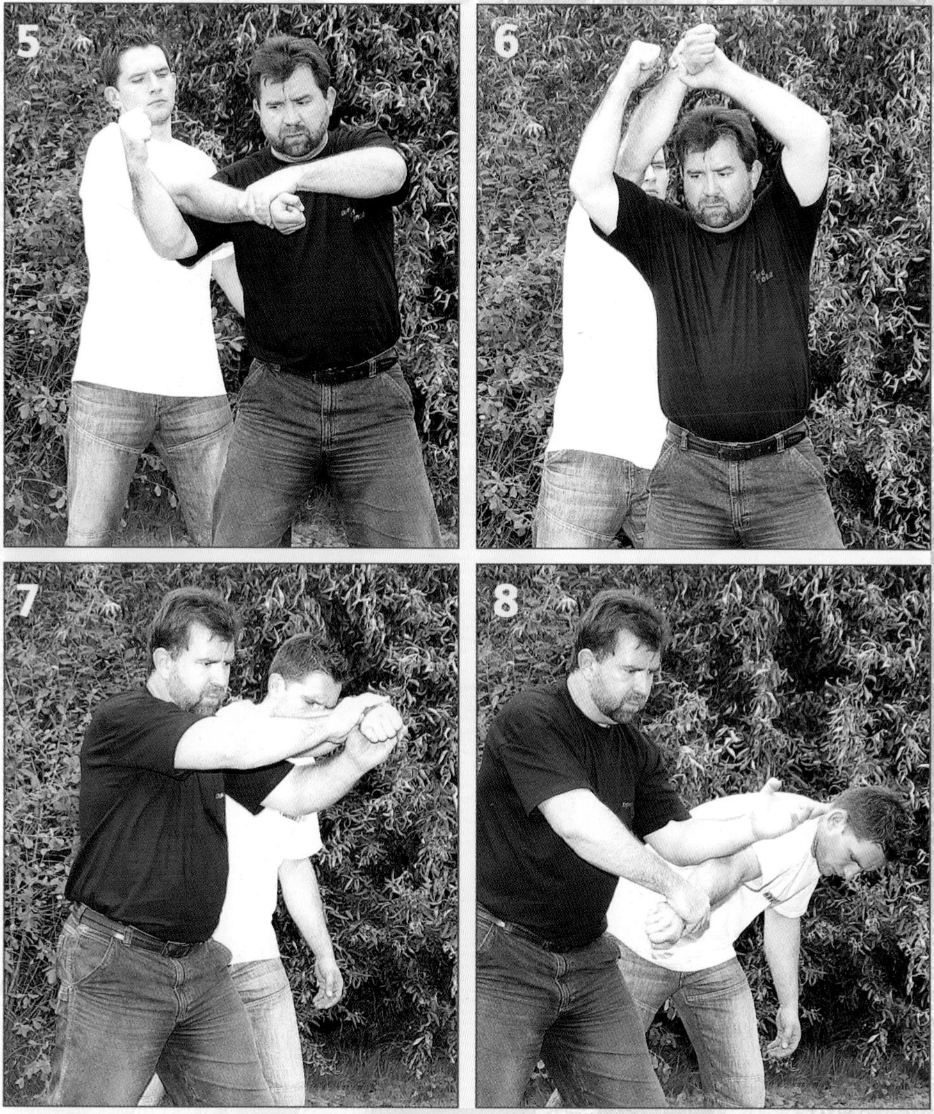

5. ...and with his right lower arm, D strikes upwards against A's right elbow joint and effects an arm breaking lock.

6. D brings A's right arm clockwise inwards over his own head with both hands...

7. ...and brings it further outwards to the left

8. ...and ends the combination with a stretched arm lock.

1. A is standing by the side of D and has laid his left arm around D's neck pressing the knife at the right hand side of D's neck.

2. D lifts his right arm up...

3. ...turns to the right...

4. ...delivers a punch using the ball of the left hand at A's face and with the right hand he takes hold of A's right wrist...

5. ...placing the left hand on the blunt side of the knife...

6. ...disarms A using his left hand.

1. A is standing behind D and is holding the knife in his right hand around in front of D's neck.
2. D grabs hold of A's weapon–bearing wrist with his right hand and presses it firmly against his own neck so that the weapon cannot be used to slice with. A would have to pull the knife to the right in order to use it. D must avoid this happening.
3. D turn inwards under A's right arm...
4. ...pulls the right arm and effects a stretched arm lock by pressing his right shoulder against A's elbow joint.
5. D disarms A using the left hand...
6. ...and gets into a safe position.

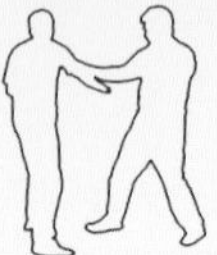

11.6 Knife attacks with the knife held as a dagger

Angle # 1: (Knife stab at the neck downward from the outside)

1. A stabs using Angle #1 at the left hand side of D's neck.
2. D blocks upwards and outwards using the edge of the hand on the left lower arm (palm down) while at the same time doing a right-handed finger jab at A's eyes.
3. D then grabs hold of the right wrist with his left hand and twists it counter-clockwise so that the flat, blunt edge of the knife is lying on his own left lower arm with the tip of it pointing upwards.
   Note: D can also sweep the weapon-bearing arm by bringing it further around counter-clockwise. This action would allow him to automatically disarm A.
4. D grabs A's right thumb in his right hand...
5. ...places the little finger of the right hand above A's forefinger...
6. ...and disarms him.

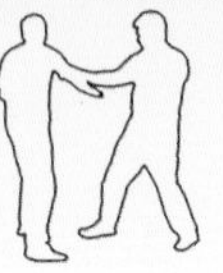

Angle # 2: (Knife stab at the neck downward from the inside)

1. A stabs using Angle #2 (downwards from the inside at D's neck).
2. D blocks upwards and outwards using the edge of the hand on the right lower arm (palm down) while at the same time doing a left-handed finger jab at A's eyes.
3. D then grabs hold of A's right wrist with his right hand...
4. ...and twists it forwards pressing the right lower arm against the blunt edge of the knife.
5. D grabs the little finger on A's right hand with his left hand...
6. ...places his own little finger of the right hand on A's little finger...
7. ...and disarms him using the right hand.

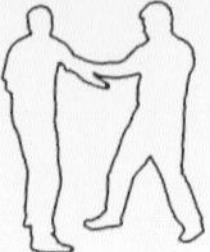

Angle # 3: (Knife stab at the stomach from the outside)

1
2
3
4
5
6

1. A stabs using Angle #3 (from the outside at stomach height)
2. D lifts the weapon-bearing arm up with his left lower arm while at the same time doing a right-handed finger jab at A's eyes.
3. D then grabs hold of A's weapon-bearing arm with his right hand...
4. ...and brings it clockwise outwards to the right...
5. ...placing the left thumb on the pommel of the knife...
6. ...and disarms him with the left hand.

Angle # 4: (Knife stab at the stomach from the inside)

1. A stabs using Angle #4 (inside at stomach height)
2. D blocks with right lower arm downwards and outwards to the right while at the same time doing a left-handed finger jab at A's head (disrupting technique).
3. D then grabs hold of the ball of A's right thumb with his left hand...
4. ...and brings A's right hand counter-clockwise outwards to the left and places the right hand on the blunt, flat side of the knife...
5. ...and disarms him with the right hand.

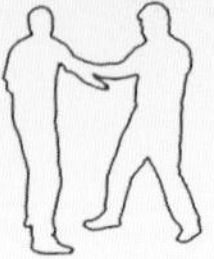

Angle # 5: (Knife stab downward at the head/upper body)

1. A stabs using Angle #5 (downward at the head/upper body)
2. D lifts the weapon-bearing arm up and brings it downwards while at the same time doing a right-handed finger jab at A's eyes.
3. D then forces A to stab himself in the thigh...
4. ...brings the arm up a little more and places the right hand on the blunt, flat side of the knife...
5. ...and disarms him with the right hand.

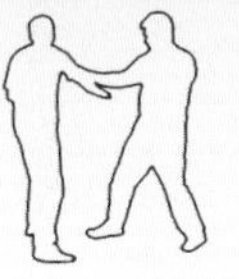

Ways of securing the knife after a successful disarming

As far as the disarming has been done using the hand, then the defender has hold of the weapon and can use it to defend himself or simply keep hold of it as a piece of evidence. If the weapon falls down to the ground, then it is sensible to pick it up straight away and keep hold of it. In a situation where you are defending yourself and there are several people around then it can be very dangerous to bend down to pick the weapon up. One of these other people could also suddenly attack you. In this case it would be better to place your foot on the weapon. This way it is also safe and cannot be used by anybody else and the defender doesn't run the risk of having to bend down and suffer a surprise attack as he picks it up. The defender should keep the weapon firmly under his foot until the attackers have gone away and it becomes safe to bend down to pick it up.

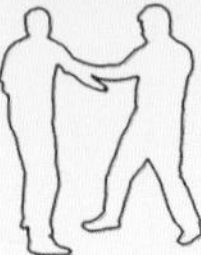

12 Unarmed Defense Against Stick Attacks

Methods of disarming a stick attack can be:

- With the hand
- With the edge of the hand
- With the lower arm
- Over the upper arm
- Over the thigh
- By striking the weapon bearing hand or arm
- Over the attacker's body

- **With the hand**

Example 1

Example 2

Example 3

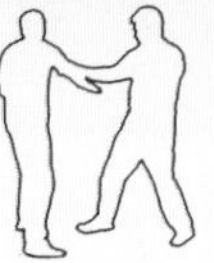

- **With the edge of the hand**

- **With the lower arm**

1

Example 1

2

Example 2

- **Over the upper arm**

- **Over the thigh**

- **By striking the weapon bearing hand or arm**

- **Over the attacker's body**

12.1 Defense against a stick attack and disarming techniques

Angle #1: (Strike comes in from the outside at the head)

1. A strikes Angle #1 (from the outside at the head).
2. D blocks using his left lower arm outwards while at the same time delivering a right-handed finger jab at the eyes.
3. D brings the right hand under A's weapon-bearing arm...
4. ...sweeps it clockwise upwards...
5. ...around and then further down grabbing the ball of A's right thumb.

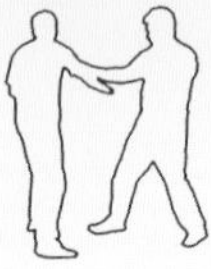

6. D strikes the stick against A's right leg...
7. ...brings A's weapon-bearing arm behind his (A's) back and places the stick on A's back.
8. D pulls A's right hand close past the right-hand side of A's body thus carrying out the disarming action.
9. D ends the combination with a stretched arm lock.

Angle #2: (Strike comes in from the inside at the head)

1. A strikes Angle #2 (from the inside at the head).
2. D blocks using his right lower arm outwards while at the same time delivering a left-handed finger jab at the eyes...
3. ...and grabbing the ball of A's right thumb in his right hand and brings A's weapon-bearing arm clockwise downwards to the left
4. D lifts his left leg up and places A's right hand directly on the outside of his own thigh.
5. D pulls A's right hand close over his thigh thus carrying out the disarming action.
6. D ends the combination with a stretched arm lock.

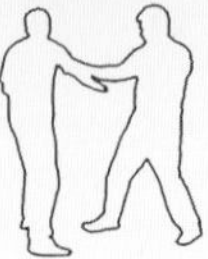

Angle #3: (Strike comes in from the outside at hip height)

1. A strikes Angle #3 (from the outside at hip height).
2. D counters with an underarm block using his left lower arm downwards and outwards while at the same time delivering a right-handed finger jab at the eyes (disrupting technique).
3. D brings the right hand over A's right arm...
4. ...sweeps it counter-clockwise to the right downward and outwards...
5. ...grabs hold of the ball of A's right thumb in his left hand...

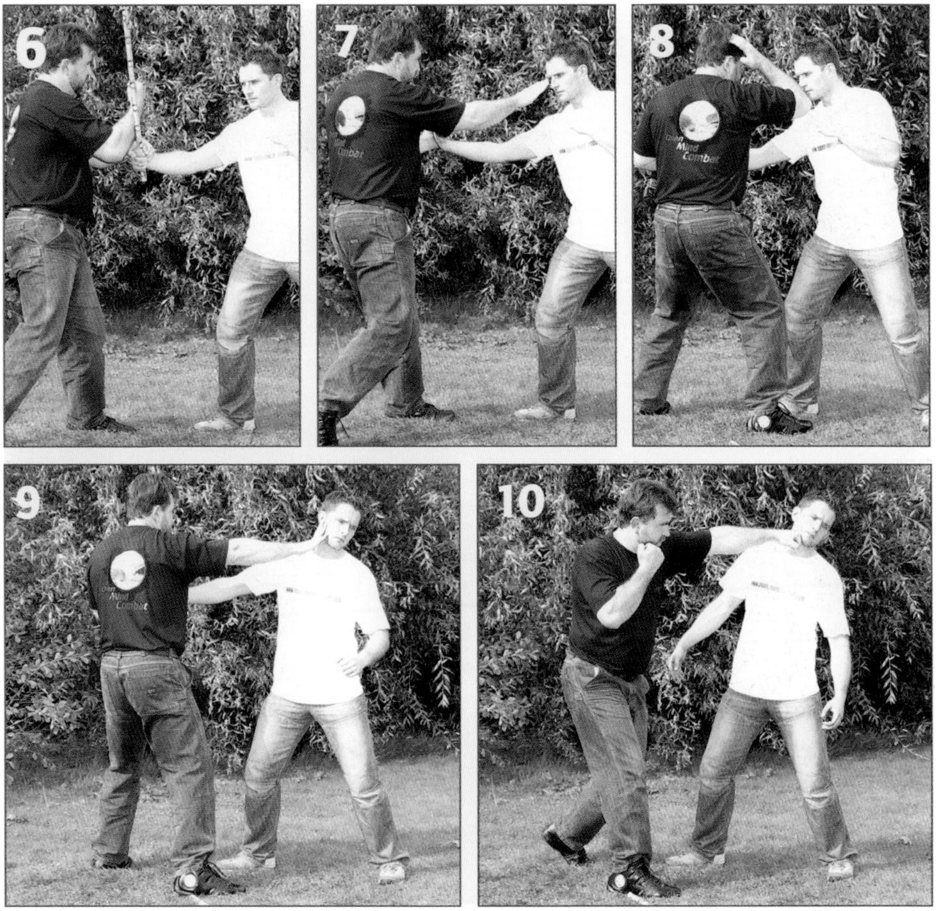

6. ...places his right lower arm on the stick...

7. ...and carries out the disarming action with the lower arm.

8. D does an elbow strike upwards at A's head...

9. ....places the right hand on the right-hand side of A's face and presses his head to the right.

10. Finally, D delivers a left-fisted punch at A's head.

Angle #4: (Strike comes in from the inside at hip height)

1. A strikes Angle #4 (from the inside at hip height).
2. D counters with an underarm block using his right lower arm downwards and outwards while at the same time delivering a left-handed finger jab at the eyes (disrupting technique).
3. D grabs hold of the ball of A's right thumb in his left hand...
4. ...twists A's right hand counter-clockwise to the left until the long part of the stick is pointing upwards, places his right hand on the stick...
5. ...and carries out the disarming action with the hand.

Angle #5: (Strike at the stomach)

1. A strikes Angle #5 (at the stomach).
2. D counters with an underarm block using his right lower arm downwards and outwards while at the same time delivering a left-handed finger jab at the eyes (disrupting technique).
3. D grabs hold of the ball of A's right thumb in his left hand...
4. ...grabs hold of the end of the stick in his right hand...
5. ...and rips the stick downwards...
6. ...thus carrying out the disarming action.

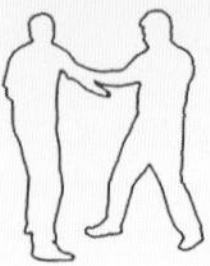

Angle #6: (Strike comes downward at the head)

1. A strikes Angle #6 (downwards at the head).
2. D counters by sweeping his hand out to the left while at the same time grabbing hold of the ball of A's right thumb and delivering a finger jab at A's eyes (disrupting technique).
3. D hits A's right leg with the stick...
4. ...brings the stick around behind A's back and places the stick between A's legs.
5. D pulls A's right hand close past and against A's right thigh thus carrying out the disarming action.
6. The combination is ended by delivering a right-fisted punch at A's head.

Angle #7: (Strike comes in from the outside at knee height)

1. A strikes Angle #7 (from the outside at knee height).
2. D sweeps the weapon-bearing arm diagonally counter-clockwise downwards and takes a step backwards with his right leg.
3. With the right hand D sweeps the weapon-bearing arm further downwards and outwards to the right while at the same time delivering a finger jab at A's eyes (disrupting technique).
4. D brings the weapon-bearing arm further counter-clockwise upwards to the right..
5. ...brings it around behind A's neck...
6. ...presses his left hand against A's head pulling A's right arm closely over his throat...
7. ...and disarms A over the body.

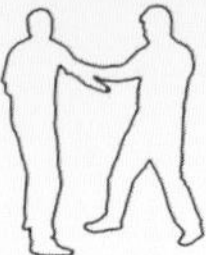

Angle #8: (Strike comes in from the inside at knee height)

1. A strikes Angle #8 (from the inside at knee height).
2. With the left hand D sweeps the weapon-bearing arm diagonally counter-clockwise downwards to the left while at the same time delivering a finger jab at A's eyes with the right hand (disrupting technique).
3. D grabs hold of A's right hand in his right hand...
4. ...twists the weapon-bearing hand clockwise to the right placing the left hand on the stick up above A's right hand...
5. ...and disarms A with the hand.

12.2 Defense against an attack by a baseball bat

Angle #1: (Strike comes in from the outside at the head)

1. A strikes Angle #1 (from the outside at the head).
2. D takes a sideways step forward with the right leg and at the same time delivers a finger jab at A's eyes with the right hand (disrupting technique) and an underarm block outwards to the left.
3. D brings his left arm counter-clockwise around both of A's arms...
4. ...brings his arm counter-clockwise upwards pulling his arm towards himself...
5. ...and disarms A with a movement forward to the left using the so-called "Snake" disarming action.
6. Following on from this, D delivers a right-fisted punch at A's head...

7. ...followed by a left-fisted punch again at the head...

8. ...and finally another right-fisted punch at the head (chain of blows).

9. D brings both of his thumbs up over A's eyes...

10. ...and grabs around behind A's neck...

11. ...and does a head butt at A's head...

12 13 14

15 16

12. ...then a knee-up kick at A's genitals.

13. D carries out a forward strike with his elbow at A's head...

14. ...twists A's head clockwise to the right...

15. ... and brings him down onto the ground.

16. D stamps down on A's head with a kick to end the combination.

Angle #2: (Strike comes in from the inside at the head)

1. A pulls the baseball bat back to gain momentum...
2. ...and strikes Angle #2 (from the inside at the head).
3. D counters using a finger jab at A's head with the left hand (disrupting technique)...
4. ...places his left lower arm onto A's right lower arm and at the same time delivers a further finger jab at A's eyes with the right hand (disrupting technique)...
5. D sweeps the weapon-bearing arm downwards...
6. ...and wraps his left arm around both of A's arms...

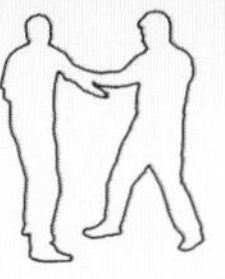

7. ...rips his left elbow up...

8. ...and disarms A with a movement using the "Snake" disarming action.

9. Following on from this, D delivers a right-fisted punch at A's head...

10. ...followed by a left-fisted punch again at the head...

11. ...and finally another right-fisted punch at the head (chain of blows).

12. D brings both of his thumbs up over A's eyes...

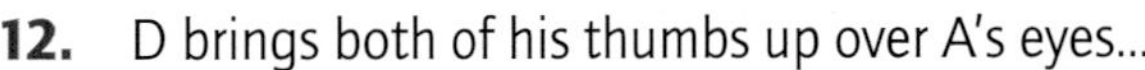

13. ...and grabs around behind A's neck...

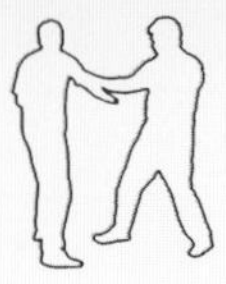

14. ...and does a head butt at A's head...

15. ...then a knee-up kick at A's genitals.

16. D carries out a forward strike with his right elbow at A's head...

17. ...grabs A's neck in both hands and...

18. ...twists A's head clockwise to the right...

19. ... and brings him down onto the ground.

20. D stamps down on A's head with a kick to end the combination.

13 Defense Using Everyday Objects

Basically you can throw any small everyday object into the attackers face in order to achieve a surprise. You can use this shock tactic to employ further techniques or even flee.

You can also throw the object over the attacker. When the attacker looks up (because he doesn't want to be struck by a flying object) this is a good moment to deliver a kick or, for example, a knee-up kick in the genitals.

13.1 Using an umbrella against a close contact attack

1. A takes D in a bear hug from the side pinning down his arms.
2. The umbrella is in D's right hand and he brings it around behind A's back and then grabs hold of it in his left hand...

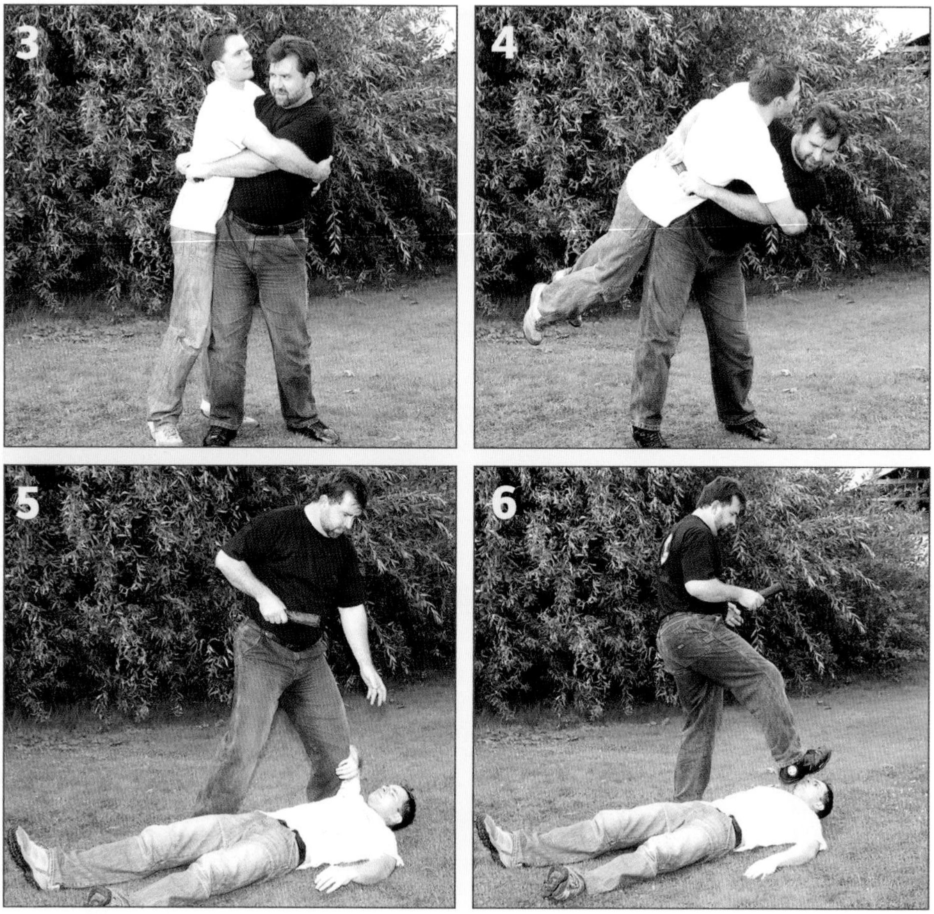

3. ...and tightens the grip firmly around A lifting up so that A has to stand on tiptoe.

4. D lifts A right up...

5. ...and throws him over his hip forward onto the ground.

6. The combination ends with a downward kick.

1. A grabs hold of D's wrist (the one holding the umbrella) diagonally with his right hand.
2. With his left hand, D pins the fingers of A's right hand against his own right wrist and at the same time kicks A's shin (disrupting technique).
3. D 'rolls' the end of the umbrella from the outside over A's wrist and carries out a twisted hand lever.
4. D takes hold of the end of the umbrella in his left hand...
5. ...and using the short end of the umbrella delivers a strike at A's chin.
6. D brings the umbrella further around over to the left-hand side to possibly carry out further strikes.

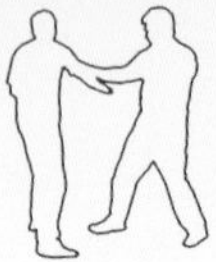

1. A grabs hold of D's wrist (the one holding the umbrella) diagonally with his right hand.
2. D 'rolls' the umbrella over A's wrist.
3. With his left hand, D grabs through under A's right arm...
4. ...grabs hold of the umbrella, carrying out a blocking hand lever.
5. D lets go of the umbrella out of his right hand (and it strikes A in the face as it whips out of the tension it was in).
6. D brings the umbrella further around over to the left-hand side to possibly carry out further strikes.

1. A grabs hold of D's wrist (the one holding the umbrella) diagonally with his right hand.
2. With his left hand, D grabs hold of A's right lower arm (near the wrist)...
3. ...twists it in a clockwise direction and achieves a freeing action with his right hand.
4. D turns A further around...
5. ...places the handle end of the umbrella on the back of A's right hand...
6. ...turns (tips) A's right wrist counter-clockwise to the left...
7. ...and brings A down to the ground using twisting hand lever (at the end of the umbrella.
8. The combination is ended with a kick downwards at the head.

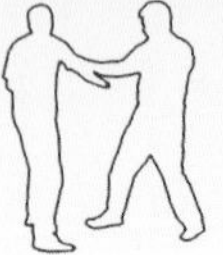

1. A grabs hold of D's right wrist (the one holding the umbrella) with his right hand opposite.
2. With his left hand, D grabs hold of the short end of the umbrella...
3. ...and brings the umbrella clockwise into a vertical position.
4. D presses his right lower arm down onto A's hand and executes a hand-blocking lever.

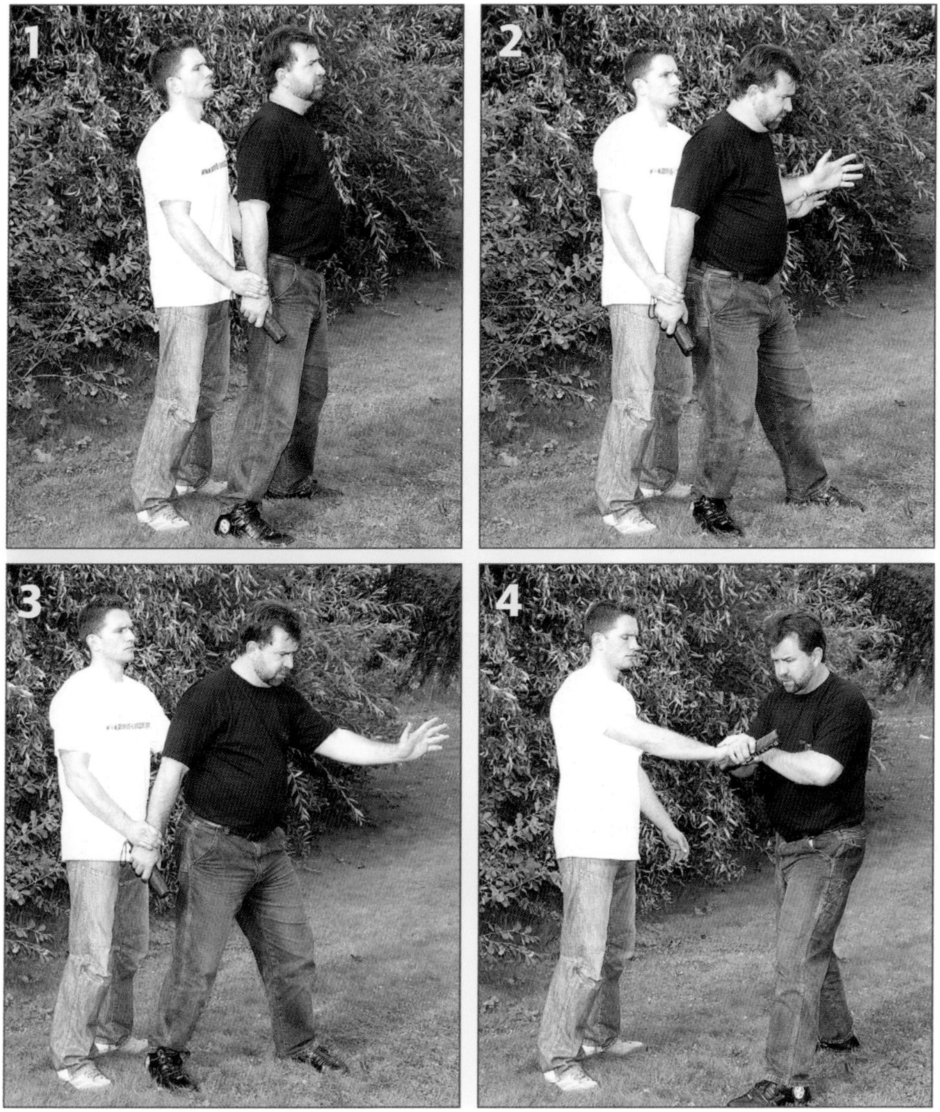

1. Standing behind D, A grabs hold of both of D's wrists.
2. D bends his left arm up from the elbow...
3. ...frees himself using the right hand holding the umbrella...
4. ...followed by a step turn 180° forwards. D pins down A's right hand with his left hand...

5. ...and executes a twisted hand lever...

6. ...bringing A down to the ground.

7. D takes the umbrella in his left hand...

8. ...and strikes A's chin with the umbrella.

9. D brings the umbrella further over to the left.

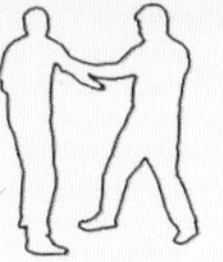

13.2 Using a newspaper against an attack without contact and with a weapon

Here, it is assumed that the defender is carrying a newspaper that has been rolled together. In this way the newspaper is so hard that it is equivalent to having a stick.

1. A strikes Angle #1 (from the outside at the head).
2. D counters by punching A with his right fist...
3. ...brings the newspaper across to his left hip...
4. ...and thrusts the short end (butt) of the newspaper at A's head...

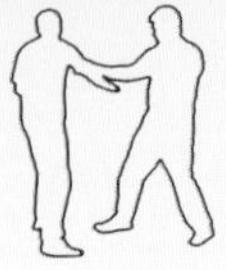

5. and then executes a quick blow (Abanico style) at A's head.

6. D brings his left arm around over A's right arm...

7. ...and then counter-clockwise further upwards...

8. ...and disarms A with the "Snake" disarming action to the left (45°).

1. A stabs at Angle #5 with a knife at the stomach.
2. Using the newspaper, D strikes the attacking arm downwards and outwards to the right...
3. ...secures A's weapon-bearing right arm with his left hand...
4. ...delivers a blow with the newspaper at A's nose...
5. ...followed by a blow using the short end of the newspaper (butt) against the weapon-bearing hand.
6. The disarming action is achieved when the blow strikes the hand.

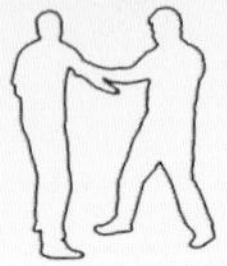

1. A stabs at Angle #1 (from the outside at the neck) with a knife held in the dagger mode.
2. D blocks with the edge of his left hand (palm down) and at the same time thrusts the newspaper at A's larynx (NB: dangerous). Then D grabs hold of A's right wrist...
3. ...twists the weapon-bearing arm counter-clockwise downwards and places his own lower arm on the flat, blunt side of the blade.
4. D places the newspaper on the blade...
5. ... and disarms A.

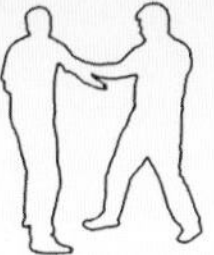

13.3 Using a vehicle key

1. A delivers a punch (swinging punch) at D's head.
2. D blocks with his left lower arm outwards to the left and at the same time jabs the vehicle key at the nose.
3. Finally D then does a knee-up kick into A's genitals.

1. A is standing in front of D and is about to push him.
2. D sweeps the attacking arm outwards using both arms...
3. ...jabs the vehicle key in the hollow below the larynx...
4. ...and ends the combination by kicking A in the genitals.

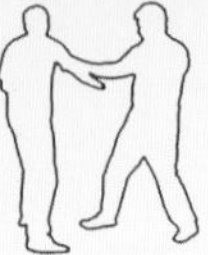

1. A takes D in a bear hug with both arms underneath D's arms.
2. D presses the vehicle key into the neck below the left ear...
3. ...then places the left thumb underneath A's nose and pushes it backward so that A loosens his grip.
4. D then ends the combination with a knee-up kick at A's genitals.

13.4 Using a book

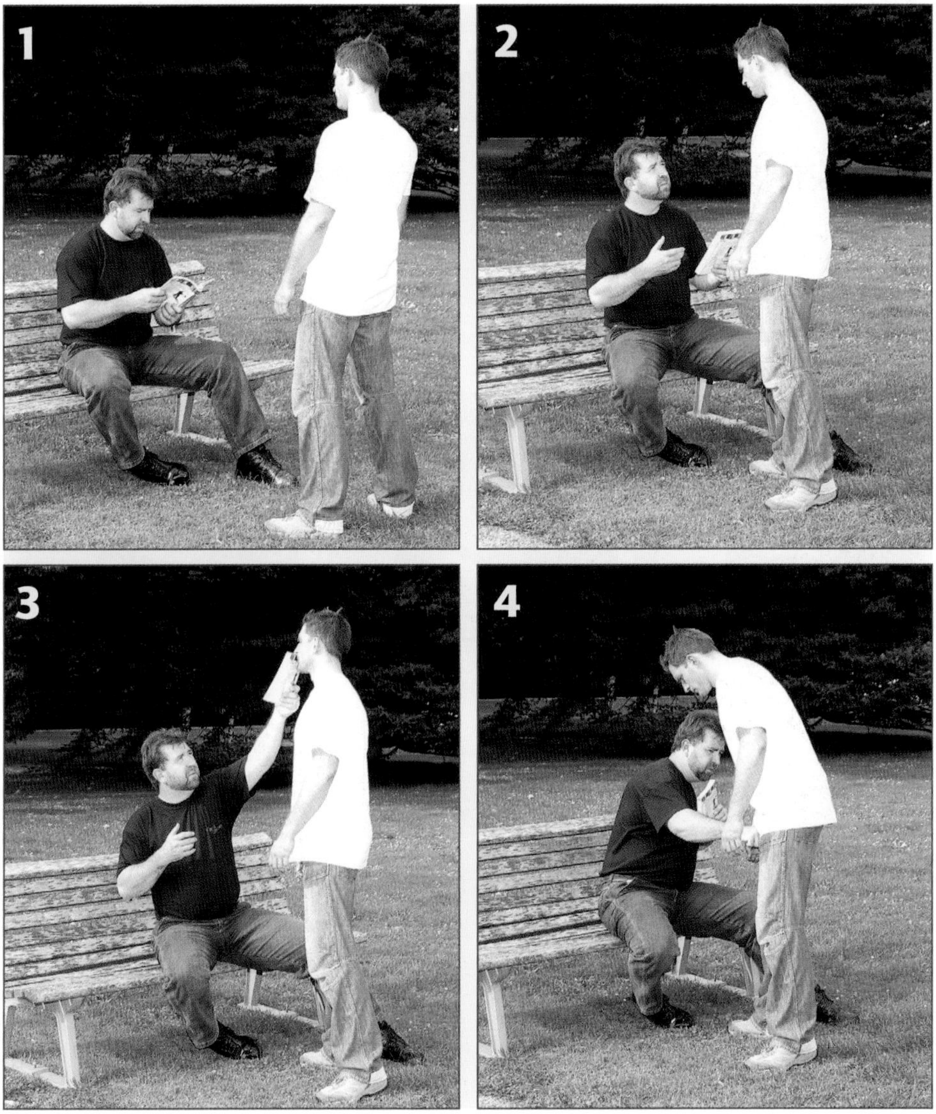

1 2 3 4

1. D is sitting on a bench reading a book.
2. A approaches him and is about to attack him.
3. D thrusts the book up and hits A's nose...
4. ...and then delivers a right-fisted punch at A's genitals.

1. A stabs at Angle #1 (from the outside at the neck).
2. D blocks with the edge of his left hand (palm down) and takes a step 45° forward with the right foot and also thrusts the book at A's larynx (NB: dangerous).
3. Then D grabs around hold of A's right arm and twists it counter-clockwise inwards
4. D places the flat, blunt side of the blade on his right upper arm...
5. ...brings the right upper arm to the left-hand side of the body thus achieving a disarming action.
6. Finally, D strikes A's nose with the book.

1. A stabs at Angle #5 (at D's stomach). D is standing in front of A and has the book open in his hand.
2. When the knife stab by A reaches the level of the book...
3. ...D shuts the book...
4. ...turns it up the other way...
5. ...and disarms A.
6. D ends the combination by doing a stamping kick downwards with the right foot at A's right thigh.

13.5 Using a ballpoint pen

1. A is standing in front of D and pushes him.
2. D sweeps the attacking arm away using both arms...
3. ...and delivers a jab with the ballpoint pen at A's nose.
4. The combination is ended with a kick in the genitals.

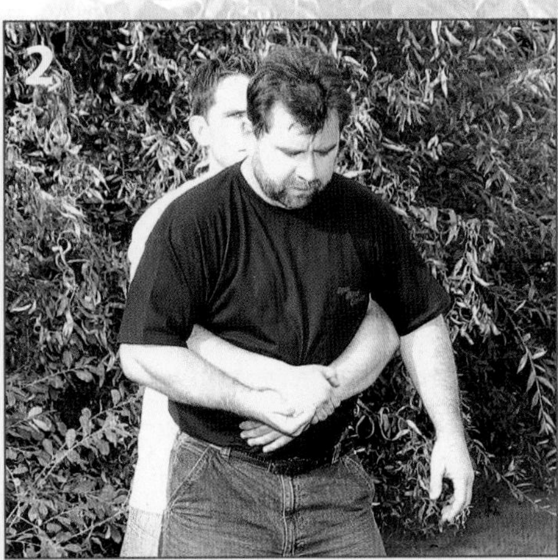

1. A is standing behind D and takes him in a bear hug with both arms underneath D's arms.
2. D delivers a jab with the ballpoint pen at the back of A's right hand so that, from the pain, A loosens his grip.
3. D twists around clockwise and does a strike backwards with the right elbow at A's head.
4. D then delivers a jab into the genitals using the ballpoint pen.
5. D then ends the combination by kicking backwards at A's midriff.

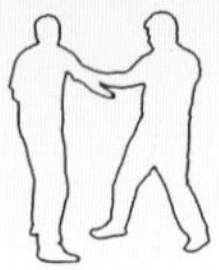

1. A strikes Angle #2 (from the inside at the head).
2. D places the left hand on the weapon-bearing arm...
3. ...sweeps the weapon-bearing arm clockwise with his left hand outwards to the left and jabs the ballpoint pen at A's eye.
4. D brings his own right hand underneath A's weapon-bearing arm...
5. ...sweeps the arm clockwise upwards and spreads his right thumb outwards...
6. ...grabs hold of the right wrist in his right hand (still holding the ballpoint pen)...
7. ...and brings A's weapon-bearing arm further clockwise outwards to the left and places the left hand on the flat, blunt side of the blade...
8. ... carrying out the disarming action.

1. A is standing in front of D and is strangling him with both hands.

2. D jabs the ballpoint pen into A's left eye...

3. ...strikes down onto A's left arm with his right arm from the outside and strikes both of A's arms away to the left.

4. D follows this up by again jabbing the ballpoint pen at the right-hand side of A's head.

5. The combination is ended with a left-legged knee-up kick at A's genitals.

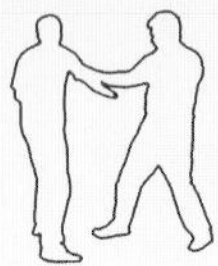

14 Close Quarter Attacks with a Pistol

As a general rule there is hardly a chance that you can defend yourself against an attack with a firearm and come away without being injured. If it is 'only' about valued objects such as a bag, watch or even the motor vehicle, it is worth considering whether the injury or even death is worth fighting for. If the attacker wants to take your watch, then I recommend, let him have it. If, however, you expect that you or other people will definitely be shot, then you can use one of the following combinations that, of course, you will have had to practice intensively before using. Talk the attacker into believing that you will do everything he says. However, you should note the following points.

14.1 Is the firearm cocked?

If the pistol (or the revolver) is cocked then the trigger pull only needs 400 g of pressure to fire the weapon, i.e. even the smallest of jolts can discharge the weapon. This is of course extremely dangerous and in my opinion no defense can be offered without danger of injury. However, if the weapon has not been cocked then the trigger pull is about 4 kg (i.e. ten times as much). In such a case, disarming becomes an option.

14.2 When should disarming take place?

You are attacked. Perhaps the attacker wants to rob you or wants (in the case of a woman) to carry out an indecent act. You wait until he starts to look or touches you. He will not be expecting a defensive reaction. At the moment that he starts to concentrate on your pockets or your body, you begin to carry out the disarming with all the courage, determination, force and speed that you can muster.

14.3 In which direction should the disarming be made?

Where possible, watch out for where other people may be standing, because you can expect that during the disarming a shot will be let off. The disarming actions in the following descriptions begin with the weapon being pushed out away to the right (as seen from D's perspective). This means that nobody should be standing on the right-hand side next to or behind D. You should also reckon with the possibility of a ricochet from a wall hitting either you or a bystander.

14.4 What is the first move in a sequence of defensive actions?

The first thing is to get out of the line of fire; for example, you have to turn your body away. If the defender concentrates on a sweeping action or a grab at the weapon, there is a large danger of being hit by a bullet. You carry out a defensive technique with the hand once the body is in a position where it cannot be hit.

14.5 Using the weapon after a successful disarming

Only the attacker knows if the weapon is real or whether it is really loaded. If, after a successful disarming, you try to use the weapon against the attacker, you can reckon on being attacked again because he will know, for example that the weapon is not loaded.

14.6 How is it possible to disarm an attacker and avoid being shot?

When the defender carries out a defensive action very quickly and precisely, the attacker's eyes follow these movements. His eye transmits the information to his brain and the brain controls the trigger finger. This sequence costs time so that a disarming can really be effective. On top of this, of course there is the surprise that can be achieved – the so-called transistory vagotonic shock phase (this can last up to 20 seconds) – during which time the attacker is unable to react.

In training I am often quicker than my exercise partner (the attacker), although he knows exactly that I am about to carry out a disarming action. In training, if he were to shoot first as soon as I move, he would generally not manage to do it before I had already got out of the line of fire.

14.7 Attack with a pistol at back height from behind

If you feel the pistol sticking into your back and you cannot touch the attacker with your free hand, then any form of defense is full of risks. However, when the attacker is going through your pockets with his free hand, then you will know whether he is holding the weapon in his left or right hand. In the combinations that follow I have depicted that the attacker is holding the weapon in his right hand.

1. A is standing behind D and is threatening him with a pistol held at D's back. D lifts his hands up...
2. ...turns around clockwise to the right bringing the right arm counter-clockwise downwards...

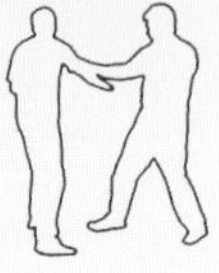

3. ...around A's weapon-bearing arm...

4. ...locks in with a bent arm lever...

5. ...and disarms A with the left hand...

6. ...and then to finish off, he strikes A's head with the butt of the pistol.

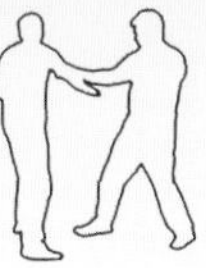

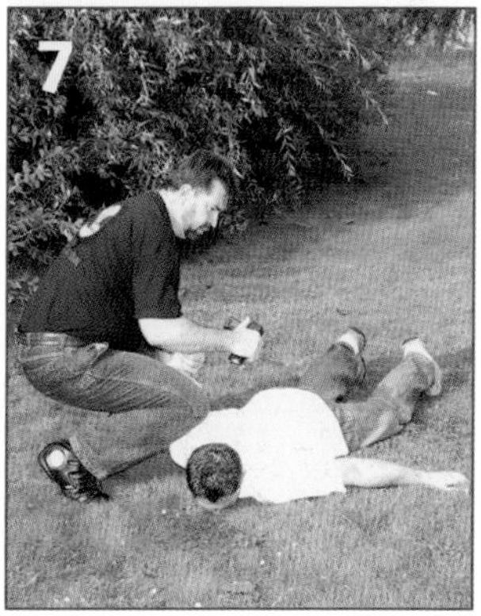

1. A is standing behind D and is threatening him with a pistol held at D's back. D lifts his hands up...
2. ...turns around counter-clockwise to the left...
3. ... bringing the left arm downwards and at the same time delivering a punch at A's larynx (Caution: dangerous for A).
4. D places his left hand on A's right elbow and then his own right hand on top of his own left hand...
5. ...does a knee-up kick into A's head...
6. ...and brings A down to the ground with a stretched arm lever...
7. ...and places his hand on the weapon and disarms A.

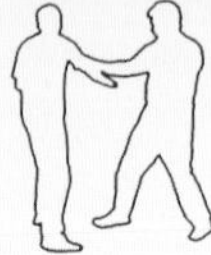

14.8 Attack with a pistol at chest height from the front

1. A stands in front of D and is pointing the weapon (with contact) at chest height. D puts his hands up...
2. ...and turns his body around clockwise...
3. ...countering by sweeping his left arm inwards.
4. D grabs hold of the weapon in his right hand...
5. ...and takes the hand in a bent hand lock. In this position D could also pull the trigger and shoot at A.
6. D brings the weapon further out to the left and carries out a disarming action.
7. D ends the combination by striking A's head with the weapon.

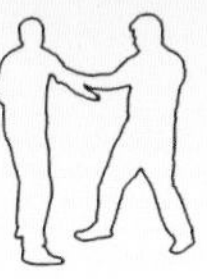

1. A stands in front of D and is pointing the weapon (with contact) at chest height. D puts his hands up...
2. ...and turns his body around clockwise.
3. With his right hand, D grabs hold of A's right wrist and at the same time he grabs hold of the barrel of the pistol in his left hand (both of D's thumbs are on top for this)...
4. D keeps hold of A's right hand with his right hand. With his left hand D twists the weapon counter-clockwise further and further to the left thus disarming A. D can now take the weapon and control A by using it. D must, however, remember that only A knows whether the weapon is real or is loaded. D shouldn't assume anything and must be prepared for a counter-attack from A.

1. A stands in front of D and is pointing the weapon (with contact) at chest height. D puts his hands up...

2. ...and turns his body around counter-clockwise...

3. ...and grabs down to hold the barrel of the pistol in his right hand...

4. ...and twists clockwise to point at A. This induces a finger lock that pulls A around.

5. D grabs the weapon in his left hand and rips it with both hands backwards so that A's forefinger is broken.

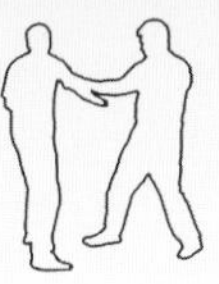

1. A stands in front of D and is pointing the weapon (with contact) at chest height. D puts his hands up...

2. ...and turns his body around clockwise grabbing A's right wrist in his left hand...

3. ...and rolls his left arm over A's right arm...

4. ...pins A's right elbow under his left armpit and executes a stretched lever lock on A's body. D grabs hold of the pistol in his right hand...

5. ...and carries out the disarming action.

14.9 Attack with a pistol at head height from the front

1. A stands in front of D and is pointing the weapon (with contact) at head height. D puts his hands up...
2. ...and turns his body around clockwise and grabs hold of A's right wrist in his left hand...
3. ...rolls his left arm over A's right arm...
4. ...pins A's right elbow under his left armpit and executes a stretched lever lock on A's body.
5. D grabs hold of the pistol in his right hand, rips the weapon downwards and carries out the disarming action.

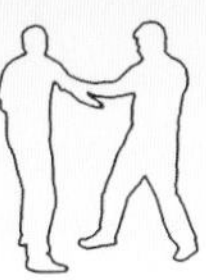

1. A stands in front of D and is pointing the weapon (with contact) at head height. D puts his hands up...
2. ...and turns his body around clockwise...
3. ...and counters by sweeping inwards to the left with the hand.
4. D grabs hold of the pistol in his right hand and carries out a bent hand lever. In this position D could also pull the trigger and shoot at A. D brings the weapon further out to the left and carries out a disarming action.
5. D ends the combination by striking A's head with the weapon.

1. A stands in front of D and is pointing the weapon (with contact) at head height [Im Original steht 'Brusthoehe' was nicht passt im Kontext]. D puts his hands up.

2. D ducks and grabs hold of A's right wrist in his left hand and the barrel of the pistol in his right hand. D keeps hold of A's right hand and pushes the barrel of the weapon upwards.

3. As soon as A loosens his grip, D twists the weapon around forwards at A and rips the weapon downwards. A's forefinger is still inside the trigger guard and jammed there so that a finger lever lock can be made.

4. D grabs the weapon in both hands, rips it over towards him breaking A's forefinger.

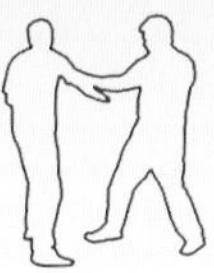

14.10 Attack with a pistol at head height from the side - The pistol is behind the right hand that is lifted up

1. A is standing on D's right side and is pointing the weapon (with contact) at head height. D puts his hands up, with his right hand in front of the weapon.

2. D turns his body around clockwise and sweeps the weapon outwards to the right with the right hand...

3. ...and grabs hold of A's right wrist with his right hand and twists A's right arm over forwards counter-clockwise.

4. D then grabs the pistol in his left hand...

5. ...and carries out a disarming action.

14.11 Attack with a pistol at head height from the side - The pistol is in front of the right hand that is lifted up

1. A is standing on D's right side and is pointing the weapon (with contact) at head height. D puts his hands up, with his right hand forward beyond the weapon.

2. D turns his head outwards and at the same time sweeps A's weapon-bearing hand forward.

3. D grabs hold of A's right wrist and puts it an arm breaking lock with his left lower arm...

4. ...carries out a kick with his knee at A's right hand with the right leg...

5. ...and disarms A.

15 Shadow Boxing/Currenza

A very effective method for improving self-defense abilities is to carry out the sequences learned without a partner in a form of "Shadow Boxing" (Currenza). It is best to do this in front of a mirror. At the beginning it might be a bit difficult but after a while you will begin to feel success. The trainee visualizes a real situation and carries out the necessary defense techniques. Music, in particular percussion instruments, can be of help in this respect, e.g. using the conga drum (Tip: CD Quem & Zaka Percussions). The trainee should adjust himself to the various rhythms and carry out the techniques in harmony with the music. You can practice combinations without using a weapon equally as well as ones with.

1

2

3

4

5

6

7

8

9

10

11

12

13

14

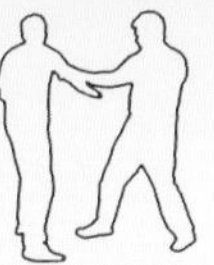

Literatur

Braun, C. (2005). *Jiu-Jitsu – the basics.* Maidenhead: Meyer & Meyer.

Braun, C. (2006). *Jiu-Jitsu – Training*. Maidenhead: Meyer & Meyer.

Braun, C. (2006). *Self-Defence against knife attacks.* Maidenhead: Meyer & Meyer.

Braun, C. (2006). *Grappling. Effective groundwork*. Maidenhead: Meyer & Meyer.

Braun, C. (2007). *Free fight – the ultimate guide to no holds barred fighting*. Maidenhead: Meyer & Meyer.

Photo & Illustration Credits

Cover Design: Jens Vogelsang
Photos: Gabi Rogall-Zelt and Jessica Rogall

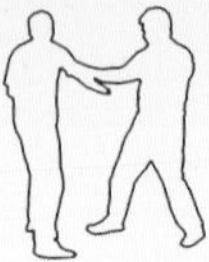

About the Author

Christian Braun, born 1965

Profession: Systems Analyst/IT Instructor

Training Address:
Fight Academy Christian Braun
Westendstraße 15
67059 Ludwigshafen
Tel.: 0049 177 2843080

Address:
Peter-Paul-Rubens-Str. 1
67227 Frankenthal
E-Mail: Christian.Braun@open-mind-combat.com
Home: www.open-mind-combat.com

Requests for information regarding courses, private training as well as books, training knives, sticks, protective glasses and martial arts accessories should be sent to the above address.

Qualifications:

- Head Instructor Open Mind Combat (OMC)
- 5th Dan Ju-Jutsu, Licensed JJ-Instructor, Trainer 'B' License
- Phase 6 and Madunong Guro in the IKAEF under Jeff Espinous and Johan Skalberg
- Instructor in Progressive Fighting Systems (Jeet Kune Do Concepts) under Paul Vunak
- Instructor in Luta-Livre License Grade 1 under Andreas Schmidt
- 1st Dan Jiu-Jitsu (German Jiu-Jitsu Association)
- Phase 2 Jun Fan Gung Fu under Ralf Beckmann

Personal Security:

- Trainer for personal security for the managing board of a big IT-Company and chemical industry in Baden-Württemberg, Germany.

Offices held:

- 1990-1991 – Trainer and Press Representative for the Ju-Jutsu Section of the Judo Association for the German State of the Pfalz (Rhineland Palatinate)
- 1999-2003 – Speaker for the Ju-Jutsu Association (Ju-Jutsu Verband Baden e.V.) in matters for Sport for Seniors and the Disabled
- 1992-today – Head of Section in the Turn- und Gefechtclub 1861 e.V. (German Gymnastics and Fencing Club 1861)

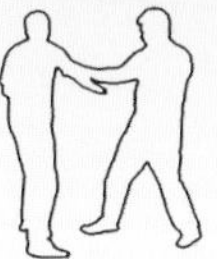

Organization:

- Speaker on the German National Seminar of the DJJV e.V. (German Ju-Jutsu Association) 2003 and 2004
- Speaker at German National Courses held by the DJJV e.V.
- Speaker in the faculty of JJ Instructors Division of the DJJV e.V.
- Member of the Trainer Team of the Ju-Jutsu Verband Baden e.V.
- Member of the Trainer Team of the DJJV e.V. in the faculty for Sport for the Disabled

Competition Achievements in the Upper Open Weight Classes:

Between 1988-1991 several place results achieved in the Pfalz Individual Championships with 1st Place taken in 1991. Placed in Third Place, three times in the German South-West Individual Championships. 2004, placed in Fourth Place in the Lock and Choke Tournament of the European Luta-Livre-Organization in the Upper Open Weight Class. In January 2005 in Karlsruhe, placed in Second Place in the Submissao Grappling Challenge. In February 2005 in Cologne, placed in SecondPlace in the Luta-Livre German Individual Championships in the Weight Class +99 kg (Advanced Class).

The Team

Gabi Rogall-Zelt

Jessica Rogall

Waldemar Wodarz

DVDs

(in German, more information and ordering possibilities: **www.fight-academy.eu**)

Braun, C. (2006). *Selbstverteidigung gegen Messerangriffe – Basics:* itf-multimedia

Braun, C. (2006). *Selbstverteidigung gegen Messerangriffe – Street Safe Workshop:* itf-multimedia

Braun, C. (2007). *Selbstverteidigung gegen Kontaktangriffe – Basics:* itf-multimedia

Braun, C. (2007). *Selbstverteidigung für Frauen – Basics:* itf-multimedia

Braun, C. (2007). *Open Mind Combat Prüfungsprogramm zur Phase I:* itf-multimedia

Braun, C. (2007). *Selbstverteidigung gegen Messerangriffe – Entwaffnungstechniken – Workshop:* itf-multimedia

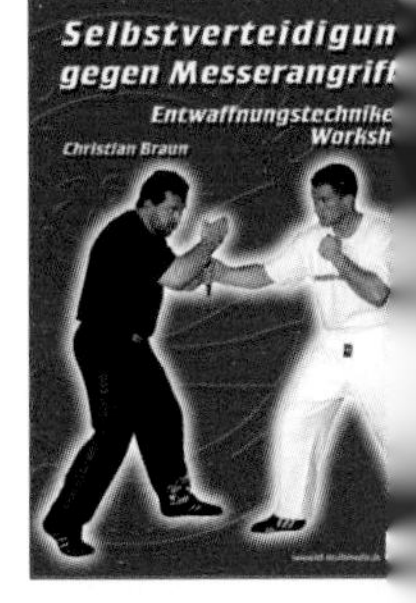

Braun, C. (2007). *Hebeltechniken – Basics:* itf-multimedia

Braun, C. (2007). *Selbstverteidigung gegen Stockangriffe – Basics:* itf-multimedia

Braun, C. (2007). *Doppelstockdrills/Sinawalis:* itf-multimedia

Braun, C. (2007). *Energydrills – Basics Energydrills – Advanced:* itf-multimedia